"In the year 793, the pagans from the north came with a force of ships to Britain, like stinging hornets." So wrote an early Saxon chronicler of the first Viking raiders to England. Ironically, much Viking history was written as propaganda by their victims in the West. European monks told alarming tales of the dreaded berserkers, or shock troops, who were reputed to bite their shields in battle fury: "Neither fire nor steel could stop them."

Yet, is this traditional Western view of the Vikings a fair one? Drawing on a wide range of chronicles, sagas, and other sources, Michael Gibson suggests a different emphasis. True, the Vikings were warlike and obsessed with fame beyond death; but Harald Hardradi could write, "At the chess board I am skilful, runic writing I know well; books I like, with tools am handy, good with snowshoes, rowing and shooting, and expert with harp and verses." Indeed, the Vikings were in many ways a refined and civilized people; good farmers and craftsmen; enterprising traders who journeyed to Constantinople; ingenious navigators who voyaged to Iceland, Greenland and Vinland without compasses; and great storytellers whose sagas have deeply influenced Western literature.

Frontispiece A modern reconstruction of the Danes attacking Ireland

The Vikings

Michael Gibson

"I'll mount my ocean steed
And o'er the hills I'll speed,
Forests and hills are not for me,
I love the moving sea."
—Snorri Sturlason.

Wayland

In this series
BATTLE OF THE SPANISH ARMADA *Roger Hart*
THE BLACK DEATH AND PEASANTS' REVOLT *Leonard Cowie*
THE BRITISH RAJ *Denis Judd*
THE HOME FRONT *Marion Yass*
MEDIEVAL PILGRIMS *Alan Kendall*
ORIGINS OF WORLD WAR ONE *R. Parkinson*
ORIGINS OF WORLD WAR TWO *R. Parkinson*
PLAGUE AND FIRE *Leonard Cowie*
THE REFORMATION OF THE SIXTEENTH CENTURY *Leonard Cowie*
THE THIRD REICH *Michael Berwick*
THE VIKINGS *Michael Gibson*
WITCHCRAFT *Roger Hart*

Cover: Detail from a twelfth-century church carving illustrating the story of Sigurd, from Hylestad in Norway.

First published in 1972 by
Wayland (Publishers) Ltd
61 Western Road, Hove
East Sussex BN3 1JD, England

2nd impression 1987

ISBN 1 85210 282 9

Printed and bound at
The Bath Press, Avon, England

Contents

The Illustrations

Introduction

"IN THE YEAR 793, the pagans from the North came with a force of ships to Britain like stinging hornets and spread out on all sides like terrible wolves, robbed, tore and slaughtered, not only beasts of burden, sheep, oxen, but even priests and deacons, and companies of monks and nuns. And they came to the Church of Lindisfarne and laid everything waste. They plundered, they trampled upon the holy places with filthy feet, they dug up the altars and seized all the treasures of the holy Church. They killed some of the monks, and took others away with them in chains; they drove many out, naked and loaded with insults, and some they drowned in the sea (1)."

The Viking homelands

Who were these people? The Saxons had no idea at this time. Later, they learned that they were Vikings or Northmen from Scandinavia—that is Norway, Sweden and Denmark. In those days, Norway was a wild country, "craggy and barren and surrounded by cliffs and huge boulders which gave it a rugged and gloomy appearance (2)." Adam of Bremen went on: "In its most northern parts the day star is never hidden, and the sun pays no attention to the change between night and day, but gives to each an equal share of its rays (3)."

Most of the people lived in long, deep valleys called fjords which opened out into the sea. A line of islands protected the mouths of these sunken valleys so that their waters were calm and sheltered; this provided ideal conditions for sailing and fishing. Along the sides and at the head of the fjords, there was a little land on which crops could be grown. The mountains were high with wooded slopes and were covered with high pastures which provided good grazing for cattle and sheep.

Sweden was an easier country to live in. The mountains were lower, and there was much more flat, cultivable land. Great forests and lakes abounded, and large rivers made their way to the Baltic Sea. The winters were much longer and harder than Norway's. The land was snowbound for five or six months a year, and the rivers were frozen solid. The people only had a short time in which to grow and harvest their crops.

Denmark consisted of the Jutland peninsula. The land was flat, and covered with poor thin soil. Denmark included some islands, such as Zealand which was "by far the most delightful of our provinces and the heart of Denmark (4)." Denmark's greatest asset was its central position between the Baltic Sea in the east and the Atlantic and North Sea in the west.

Reasons for the raids

All this helps to explain why the Vikings went raiding. There was so little good farm land available that even a slight increase in the size of the population produced serious food shortages and forced them to look for new lands to settle. Some Vikings fled from Scandinavia to escape from the tyranny of their rulers; others because they had committed serious crimes. But these were relatively few in numbers.

The search for trade led the Vikings to many new lands, including Russia. Wherever there were recognized trade routes, there were easy pickings for bold pirates like many of the Vikings.

Finally, the whole Viking view of life called for daring, adventurousness and agression. Every man sought to prove himself a hero, and found in war the greatest test of all.

Charles the Great

The Vikings were well equipped: their ships (Chapter 4) and weapons (Chapter 1) were the finest in Europe. Moreover the time was ripe. Charles the Great (768–814) had created a large and powerful empire, but even before his death cracks had appeared in its defences; Charles' biographer described an early Viking attack and the Emperor's reaction to it:

"Once, while he was on a journey, Charles came unannounced to a certain town which lies on the seashore in Southern Gaul [France]. While he was eating his supper, a party of Northmen attacked the harbour. When their ships first appeared, some people thought they were Jewish traders, others that they were Africans or traders from Britain but Charles knew better. From the trim of the ships and their speed through the water, he knew them to be warships rather than merchant vessels. 'Those ships are not filled with friendly merchants,' he said to his men. 'They contain savage enemies.'

"When they heard this, the soldiers raced at top speed towards the ships, each trying to reach them first. They were not successful, for as soon as the Northmen learned that the man they called Charles the Hammer was in the neighbourhood, they sailed away as fast as they could.

"Charles, who was a Godfearing, just and devout ruler, rose from the table and stood at a window looking east. For a long time tears poured down his face, but no one dared to ask him why. In the end he said, 'My faithful servants, do you know why I was crying so bitterly? I was not afraid that these ruffians would do me any harm, but was sick at heart to think that they dared to attack this coast in my lifetime, and was filled with horror when I thought of the evil they will do my descendants and their subjects.' (5)."

Early raids

Charles did well to worry, because the Vikings were already on the move. Farmers from south-west Norway were settling in the Orkneys and Shetlands, and sending out raiding parties to Scotland and Ireland. In the 840s, an Irish chronicler complained:

"The Vikings spread all over Ireland. They built so many fortresses and harbours that there is nowhere in all Ireland without their pirate fleets. They conquered her. They pillaged her lands, her churches and her sanctuaries and destroyed her shrines, her holy relics and her books. In fact, one can no more record the number of her miseries than one can count the sands of the sea, the grass in the fields or the stars in the heavens (6)."

And this was only the beginning.

Statue of a Viking warrior in Reykjavik, Iceland

1 *Warriors and Weapons*

"THE VIKINGS are a mighty nation with huge bodies and great courage. They do not know the meaning of the word defeat—they never turn their backs on their enemies but slay or are slain. It is customary for each warrior to carry with him some craftsman's tools such as axe, saw, hammer and so on, while he is wearing his armour. He fights on foot with spear and shield. He wears a sword and dagger and has a throwing spear slung across his back (7)." This is how the Vikings appeared to an Arab traveller.

Swords

Their swords were long, broad, two-edged, iron weapons. They produced strong and flexible blades with wavy patterns by twisting together several bars of iron and beating them flat. Blades made in this way did not shatter on striking iron helmets and shield rims. They had short, cross-shaped guards to protect the fingers. Often, their hilts were inlaid with gold and silver. Heavy triangular or semi-circular pommels counter-balanced the weight of the blades.

These swords were things of beauty as well as dealers of death. They were highly prized and passed down from father to son. Many of them had their own names: "King Magnus was armed with a sword called 'Leg-biter'; its guards were made of walrus ivory and its hilt was covered with gold (8)."

The Vikings hacked and slashed with their swords, and only occasionally stabbed at their opponent's throat or body. Strength and skill were required: "In the old days when men fought in battle, they did not strike fast and furiously, but took their time and picked their strokes carefully so that they were few but terrible. More regard was given to the weight of each blow than to the number struck (9)."

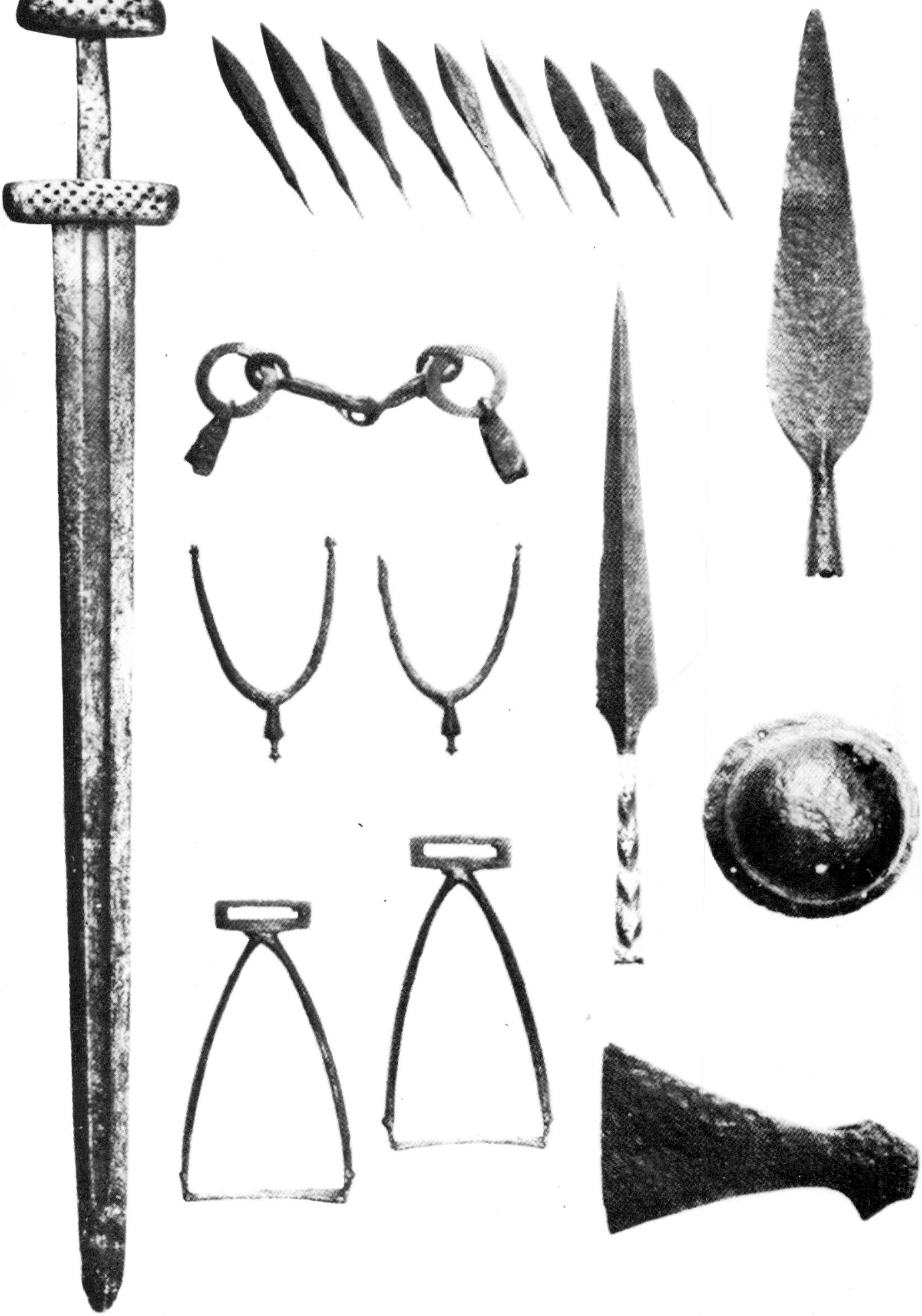

The battleaxe was the Vikings' favourite weapon. It had a large, curved blade and a four foot long shaft. Its cutting edge was made of specially hardened metal and was welded onto the rest of the blade. Its fearful power is described in Njal's Saga:

Battleaxes

"Skarp-Hedin raced down to the river, axe in hand. On the far side of the river, the ice had formed a slight mound which was as slippery as glass. On this mound stood Thrain and his men. Skarp-Hedin gathered himself and sprang straight across the river, steadied himself on landing and slid on, skimming along the ice like a bird. Just as Thrain was putting on his helmet, Skarp-Hedin swept up to him. He swung up his axe and crashed it down on Thrain's head splitting it down to the jaws and spilling his back teeth onto the ice. This all happened so fast that Skarp-Hedin was past them before anyone had time to strike back at him (10)."

The heavy spear with a leaf-shaped blade was their third weapon. It was used for stabbing and thrusting, and was called. "The flying dragon of the wounds;" "The serpent of the battle;" "The sounding fish of armour (11)." They also had lighter, throwing spears.

Spears

Left Viking shield made of wooden boards bound by iron bars *right* Viking bronze sword guard

The bow and arrow completed their armament. No bows or arrow shafts have survived to the present day, but large numbers of arrow heads have. Experts are not sure whether they used long or short bows, but their arrow heads fitted to modern shafts have great penetrating power when shot from either.

Bows and arrows

The Vikings' main defence was a round or rectangular shield,

Shields

Left Viking two-edged sword, arrow, spear and battleaxe heads, shield boss, stirrups, oarlocks and bridlepiece

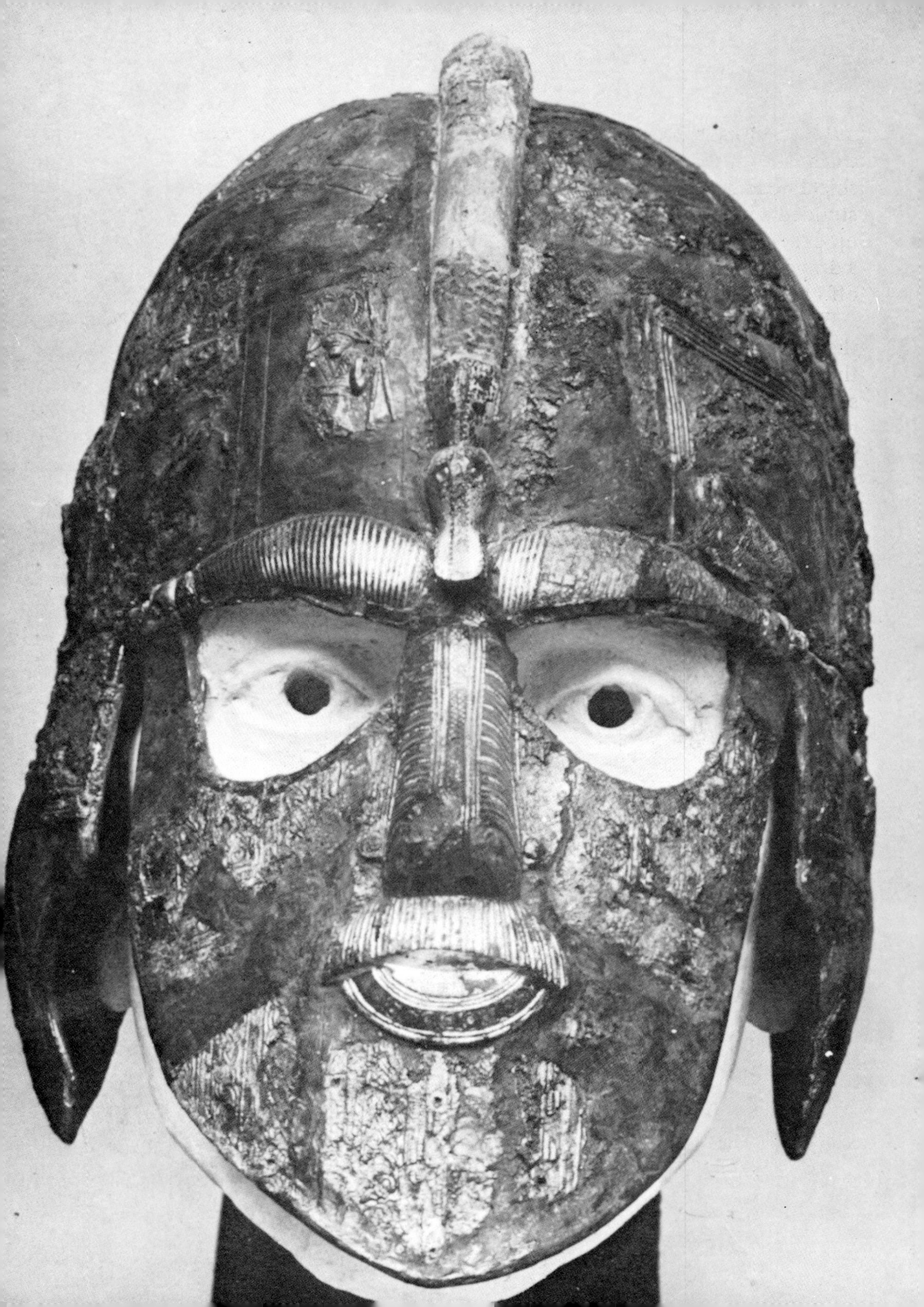

made of wooden boards, and bound together by iron bars. A round casing called a boss protected the fingers, and helped to bind the shield together. Its outer surface was covered with leather and studded with nails. It could be decorated: "Sigurd's shield was made up of several layers and was covered in red gold. On it was painted a dragon (12)." It was light and strong so that its owner could ward off blows with it, or smash it into his opponent's face.

Helmets

Their heads were protected by conical helmets, usually without the horns and wings so often portrayed by modern artists. Sometimes nose and cheek pieces were added for good measure. The saga writers often speak of them: "He wore a helmet on his head and had a sword at his side; he carried a shield and bore a spear in his hand (13)."

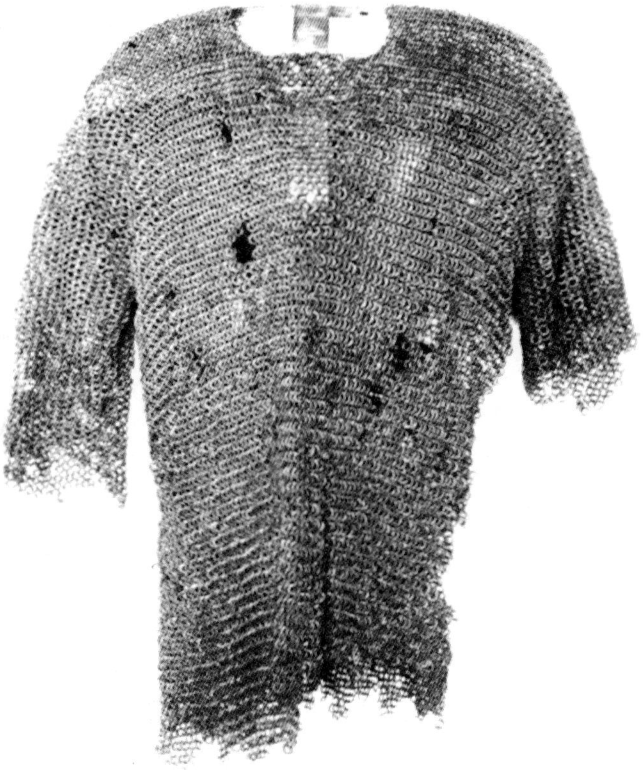

Viking mail shirt, worn as part of armour over a leather tunic

Left A Viking helmet

Overleaf A reconstruction showing Vikings landing in England

Coats-of-mail Many Vikings owned *byrnies* (mail shirts) made up of thousands of interlocking rings. These coats-of-mail repelled the blades of swords, daggers, spears and even axes, but they could not prevent deep bruising, the crushing of flesh and the smashing of bones. Leather tunics were worn under the mail to give extra protection and to stop the metal rings from rubbing the wearer's shoulders raw. With such a defence, men could afford to be brave like the Viking Hjalmar, who said: "I want to fight, for I have a byrnie in which I have never been wounded; it has four layers of rings (14)."

Horse's harness Although the Vikings usually fought on foot, they were expert riders. Their horses' furniture—the stirrups, bridles, saddles and collar harnesses—were often lavishly decorated: "They sent out messengers to search for King Sigurd. They took his horse which was provided with a gilded saddle and bridle which were set with precious stones (15)."

Armies The Vikings were not well disciplined fighters, although some generals like Olaf the Stout tried to organize them: "We have a large army and excellent troops. Now, I will tell you how our force will be drawn up. My banner will go forward in the middle of the army. I will have the people divide themselves into separate groups of friends and relations so that they will defend each other well. We shall recognize our men by the white crosses painted upon their helmets and shields. When the battle starts we must all use the same battlecry, 'Forward, forward Christian men!' Now, let the men divide themselves into groups and ranks. Let every man take note of his proper place and of the banner under which he is going to fight. Our men will remain fully armed night and day until the battle is fought (16)."

Berserkers But most battles were confused affairs, won by surprise and ferocity rather than by strategy and tactics. The shock troops were the *berserkers*, who "advanced without mail shirts and were frenzied like mad dogs and wolves—they bit their shields in their fury. They were as strong as bears or wild boars and struck men down right and left. Neither fire nor steel could stop them (17)."

Camps: Trelleborg In their own countries, the Vikings built fine camps like the one discovered at Trelleborg in West Zealand. The earthworks at Trelleborg formed a perfect circle, pierced by four tunnel-gateways. The camp was divided into four by two roads linking the gates.

Viking soldiers building earthworks

Each area contained a barracks consisting of a large hall in which 75 men lived, and smaller storerooms for their food and equipment.

Trelleborg was probably a base for one of Swein Forkbeard's fleets. It was planned and constructed with a skill worthy of the Romans; indeed, the Vikings may have learned how to build these camps from soldiers who had served in the armies of the Byzantine emperors.

The Vikings built much smaller and simpler forts in the lands they invaded: "They raised a great earthwork. Large ditches were dug and inside them they threw up ramparts of stone, timber and turf. A strong army was stationed inside (18)."

Siege warfare

Walled towns presented the Vikings with a real challenge to their military skill. At first, they could do little more than make camp outside and starve the inhabitants into submission. However, it was not long before they learned all the techniques of siege warfare so that no town was completely safe (Chapter 6).

Nevertheless, their greatest successes were achieved by guile rather than method as this account from Harald Hardradi's Saga shows: "When he came to Sicily, he plundered the countryside until he came upon a large town. He surrounded it but saw that the walls were so thick that they could not be breached. Moreover, the townspeople had ample stocks of every kind of provision. Then, he had an idea. He ordered his men to trap the little birds that flew out of the town each day to find food for their young in the woods. Once this was done, he told them to tie splinters of tarred wood to their backs and set fire to them. As soon as the birds were released, they flew straight home to their babies who lay in nests under the eaves of the houses which were thatched with straw or reeds. Although each bird only carried a tiny flame, there was soon a mighty blaze as one house after another burst into flames. At last, the townspeople came out and begged for mercy. Harald spared their lives, and took possession of the town (19)."

2 The Viking Settlements

WHAT DID THE VIKINGS look like? "Blond was his hair and bright his cheeks. Grim as a snake's were his eyes." "He was handsome and had a light complexion, a straight nose, keen blue eyes and red cheeks. His hair was long, thick and yellow and sat well on his head." "He had fine features with beautiful eyes and a fair complexion; his hair was as fine as silk and fell down in locks. He was tall and strong and better shaped than any man (20)." Friend and foe alike describe their blue eyes and blond hair. Occasionally, a "black" Viking is mentioned, one having black hair and dark eyes.

Vikings' appearance

Viking women were usually blue-eyed with long golden hair and pale skins: "Helga was so beautiful, that wise men said there was not her equal in Iceland. Her hair was so long that it could cover her whole body, and was as fine as gold." "She was fair to look at. She wore her long, fair hair loose as is the custom of maidens and had beautiful hands with many rings on them (21)."

Clothing

Their everyday clothes were simple and serviceable. The men wore long-sleeved woollen shirts and trousers with socks attached, sleeveless jerkins or tight waisted, three-quarter length coats and tall, leather boots. The women wore long, plain woollen dresses over linen petticoats, woollen socks and soft leather shoes like moccasins. Outside the house, they wore aprons over their dresses and kerchiefs over their heads. The women wore a great brooch at the shoulder from which hung scissors, keys, needle-and-thread cases, and other items. Both sexes wore thick, heavy cloaks and fur hats in cold weather.

On special occasions, their costume was much more elaborate. Here is a description of a great warrior: "He was wearing a blue tunic with a silver belt, blue striped trousers and black top boots. He was carrying a small round shield which he called 'Battle Troll'. His hair was combed well back from his forehead and held in place by a silk band. He looked every inch a warrior (22)."

The men either wore very full baggy trousers or skin-tight "drainpipe" pants. These could cause trouble: "Snorri's servant tried to pull off the wounded man's trousers and grumbled, 'They weren't lying when they said that you sons of Thorbrand are vain, your breeches are so tight that I can't pull them off.' (23)"

Fashion

A king advised his young men to dress in the following manner if they wanted to be fashionable: "You should wear long, cloth stockings of brown or any colour other than scarlet. Wear brown, green or red tunics made out of good quality cloth. Make sure that your linen clothes are made of the finest material. Always have your shirt cut short, much shorter than your trunk. Take care of your beard and hair; when I was a young man it was fashionable to have one's hair cut so that it hung level with one's earlobes and to comb it out straight. We had fringes that reached down to our eyebrows and our beards and moustaches were kept short (24)."

The women loved rich fabrics such as Chinese silks and brocades and velvets from Byzantium and the Arab empire. They chose strong colours and had their clothes cut to flatter their figures: "She sat there very conscious of her beautiful white arms. She pulled down her veil, straightened her sleeves and smoothed down

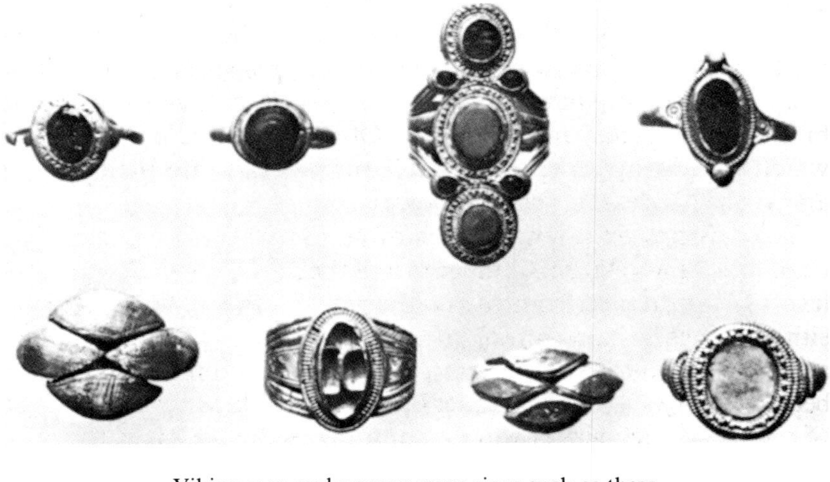

Viking men and women wore rings such as these

A hut in Iceland similar to the sort used by the Vikings

her mantle. She wore a beautiful brooch on her breast and her blue silk dress had a long train (25)."

"She was beautifully dressed in a long-sleeved red gown which was pinched in at the waist and reached right down to the ground. Her hair was very fine and was held in place by a band round the forehead (26)."

Cosmetics

Both men and women wore cosmetics, as an Arab visitor to Denmark observed: "They put an artificial make-up on their eyes and claim that if you use it your looks never fade but that on the contrary the appearance of both men and women is improved (27)."

Jewellery

Both wore ornaments of all kinds such as rings, bracelets, brooches, diadems, and necklaces. Often they were made of gold which the Vikings called "the fire" and worked into the shape of animal heads, leaves, vines or flowers.

Houses and halls

The Vikings built long houses of 40 to 100 feet in length. The foundations were deep, so that most of the house was below ground level and protected from the cold weather. The walls were made either of logs laid one on top of another, or of planks, or of wattle and daub. Two rows of wooden pillars were driven into the floor of beaten earth and joined together by tiebeams. These bore the weight of the roof which was covered with shingles, thatch or turf.

Inside there was one long room where the people sat and slept upon raised platforms running the length of the building. In the middle of the room was a fire pit. The floor was strewn with sweet smelling rushes which were changed regularly before they were trodden into a compost. The walls were hung with tapestries to keep out the draughts, and decorated with shining weapons and shields. The hall was dark; it had no windows, and the smoke from the log fire had to escape through a hole in the roof.

Little furniture was used. The men sat on benches or leaned against the walls, the women squatted on their heels. Usually there was only one chair or high seat and this was placed in the middle of the west wall facing the rising sun: "It was an ancient custom in Norway, Denmark and Sweden to have doors at each end of the hall with the high seat in the middle of the long bench facing

A Viking long house

towards the sun. The Queen sat on the left hand of the King; the seats next to them on either side were for those of the highest rank and those near the doors for the lowest (28)."

At first, the hall had to accommodate everybody, including some farm animals. But as the Viking Age proceeded improvements were made. Outbuildings were erected for the animals. The hall was enlarged; a kitchen was added at one end, and woman's room at the other. Sleeping spaces were also partitioned off.

Sauna baths

Outside every hall was found a bathhouse containing a stone oven. This oven was heated until it was red hot and then doused with water to produce steam. The Vikings lay or sat on wooden benches and sweated in the steam. When they had had enough, they completed their bath by diving into a nearby cold pool or stream. In the winter, they rolled in the snow instead.

A Viking bed used by a chief, from the Gokstad treasures, Norway

We can catch a glimpse of life in the long house in this extract from Grettir's Saga: "It was the custom in those days for the farmsteads to contain large halls. The men would sit by the long fires in the evenings and tables would be set up in front of them at mealtimes. Afterwards they lay down and went to sleep close to the fires. During the day, the women worked at their wool there (29)."

Food

The main items in the Vikings' diet were wholemeal bread made from rye and oats, porridge containing oatmeal and barley, eggs,

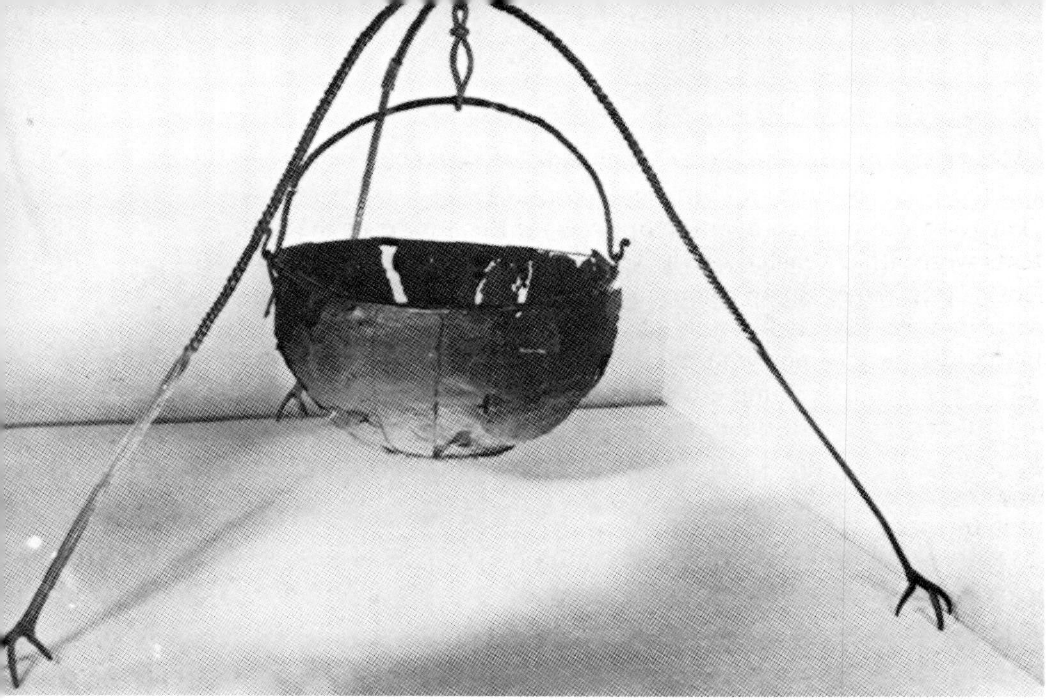

Above A Viking cooking pot and tripod. *Below* A decorated Viking hunting horn

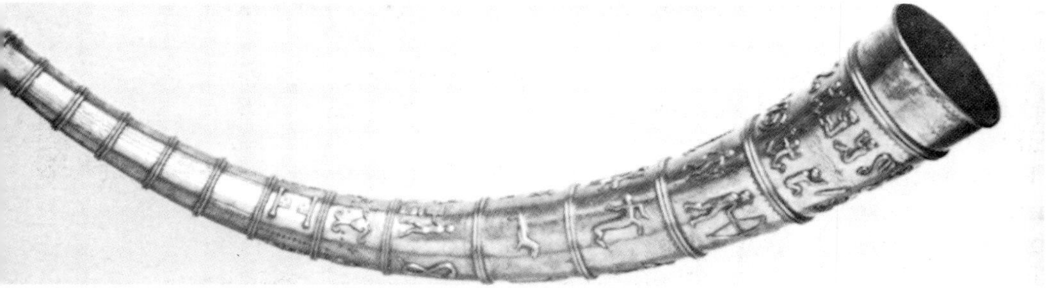

milk, cream, butter and cheese. They ate mutton, goats' flesh, horseflesh, beef and pork; in the far north, the meat of reindeer, polar bears, whales and seals could be obtained. Herring, haddock, cod and eels were favourite delicacies. The most commonly eaten vegetables were cabbages, wild greens, and onions. For fruit they had apples and all kinds of berries and nuts.

They drank great quantities of milk, buttermilk and whey, as well as a weak beer brewed from barley and a much stronger mead made from fermented honey and water. Many kinds of wine were imported from Europe and faraway Byzantium.

The food was cooked over the open fire in the middle of the hall. Meats were either roasted on the spit, boiled in great cauldrons or fried in deep pans. Bread and oatcakes were baked on flat stones laid across the firepit. In some of the ruined halls, archaeologists have found stone ovens where food was cooked between layers of red hot stones. The Vikings enjoyed plain food and preferred boiled to roast or fried meat—the heroes in Valhalla feasted off boiled pork. They loved rich stews made up of all the scraps and leftovers. Their food was sweetened with honey and flavoured with pepper and many other spices, imported from the East.

Meals

Meals were usually simple: "The tables were laid, and bread and butter and large bowls of curds were set out. They were very thirsty and drank the curds in great draughts. Then Bard had buttermilk brought in, and they drank that too (30)."

Most meals were eaten without ceremony. Feasts called for more elaborate preparation: "The lady of the house spread an embroidered cloth of white linen on the table and placed loaves of white wheaten bread on it. Then, she set out many dishes of fine ham and roasted fowls as well as silver jugs containing wine. They ate, drank and talked until the day was done (31)."

Knives and spoons were commonly in use but there were no forks. The diners ate off wooden platters or hunks of bread, and drank from tankards or drinking horns.

Farming

Farming took much of the time of most Vikings. They grew rye, barley and oats in small homefields which were enclosed by dry stone walls. After the crops had been harvested, the animals were driven into the fields to eat up the stalks and manure the ground with their droppings. Only in this way could they grow one crop of cereals after another without exhausting the soil. They had small vegetable patches and orchards of apple trees.

Between seasons, they could go raiding: "It was Svein's custom to stay at home all through the winter. In spring time, he worked hard and sowed great quantities of seed, but as soon as the work was done, he went a-viking and raided the Scottish Islands and Ireland—he called this his spring viking. At mid-summer, he returned home and stayed there until all the corn had been harvested.

Then, he went a-viking again and did not return until the first month of winter was past—he called this his autumn viking (32)."

Domesticated animals

They bred sheep, goats, cattle and chickens. The cattle were by far the most important as they provided so much of their food as well as hides for boots and clothes. As soon as the snows melted in the spring, the women and children drove the cattle up onto the mountain pastures or saetor to graze. This extract from Egil's Saga explains why:

"Skallagrim was a hardworking man. His cattle found their own food during the winter in the forests, but in summer they were taken up into the mountains. He found that those animals who went up to the pastures became much fatter than those that stayed behind (33)."

The women and children lived in little stone cottages called *shielings* where they churned the milk into butter and cheeses. In the autumn, the herd was driven down to the croplands again. Then at the beginning of winter, most of the animals were slaughtered, as there was only enough fodder for the breeding stock.

Hunting

When the men were not farming and raiding, they went out hunting for elk, wild boar, deer and even bear. In summer, they needed to keep their wits about them as the animals melted into the forest. But in winter they tracked them more easily by following their spoor in the snow. Fowling was another favourite pastime, and source of food.

Fishing

Much of their time was spent fishing in the fjords or the sea. They caught herring in the Baltic, cod and haddock in the Atlantic, and whales, seals and walruses in the cold northern seas. A Norwegian merchant called Ottar told King Alfred of England about his whaling expeditions:

"He said his main reason for sailing to the northern tip of Norway was to hunt certain whales [probably walruses] whose teeth were valuable as ivory and whose skins made fine ropes. This kind of whale is much smaller than the others as it is only about seven ells long. He said that the best whaling took place in his own area (Helgeland in Norway), because you could catch whales forty-eight ells long—the biggest reached fifty ells in length. He remembered killing as many as sixty in two days working with five other crews (34)." (An ell was a Viking measurement of just over a yard.)

They collected seaweed and spread it over their fields as a manure. Seaweed was also stored and given to the cattle during the winter, and when times were bad, the Vikings ate it themselves.

Most farmers forged their own tools and weapons, distilled tar from resinous woods, tanned skins for boots and clothing and boiled seawater to obtain salt.

Towns and trading

Many Vikings were traders and made their way to the market towns of Scandinavia such as Skiringsal in Norway, Birka in Sweden

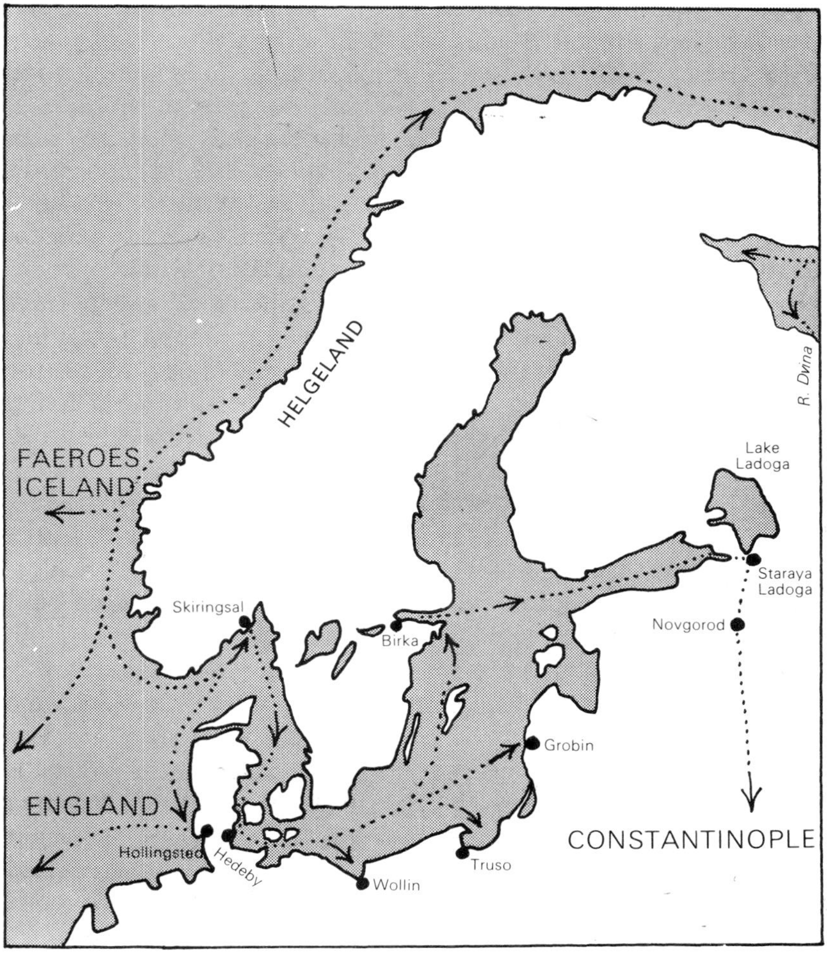

Viking towns and trade routes

and Hedeby in Denmark: "Thrand went south to Denmark and reached Hedeby in the summer. Many people were gathered there and it is said that more people go there than to any other place in the North while its fair lasts (35)."

Hedeby was the wonder of the North. It covered some sixty acres, and had a great ditch and mound to protect its landward approaches, and a solid mole to defend its harbour. It was full of large buildings, workshops, warehouses and barns as well as homes, all standing in their own grounds. The river that flowed through the city was crowded with boats. Craftsmen manufactured fine swords, blew glass, smelted silver and minted coins.

Hedeby was the focus of all the northern trade routes. Ships arrived from Western Europe, the Atlantic colonies, the Baltic lands and Russia as well as Scandinavia. And yet to an Arab visitor in the tenth century, it seemed a miserably poor and squalid town: "Hedeby is a very large town at the furthest end of the World Ocean. All its inhabitants worship a god called Sirius except for a few Christians who have a church there. They hold a festival there when everybody assembles to worship their god and to eat and to drink. When anybody sacrifices an animal, he hangs its body on a pole outside his door so that the passers-by will know. The town is badly off for food and trade goods. The people's staple food is fish, as there is so much of it. If a child is born there, it is thrown into the sea to save bringing it up. The women have the right to declare themselves divorced and leave their husbands whenever they feel like it. Their singing is the most horrible I have ever heard—it sounds like the howling of a dog, only much worse (36)."

Despite what a sophisticated Arab thought about Hedeby, the Vikings were great traders who founded many new ports and occupied and developed old ones wherever they went.

Thralls, Karls and Jarls

From very early times, the Northmen were divided into three classes:

"The *Thrall* [slave] had a swarthy skin, wrinkled hands, swollen knuckles, thick fingers and an ugly face. He had a broad back and long heels. He used his strength to bind last, make loads, and carry home faggots. His children busied themselves building fences, manuring the ground, tending the pigs, herding the goats and digging up peat.

"The *Karl* [yeoman farmer] was red and ruddy with rolling eyes and took up breaking oxen, making ploughs, building houses and making carts.

"The *Jarl* [chieftain/aristocrat] had yellow hair, his cheeks were rosy and his eyes were as keen as a young serpent's. He occupied himself shaping shields, shooting with bow and arrow, hurling the javelin, riding horses, throwing dice, fencing and swimming. He waged war, reddening the battlefield with blood and killing the damned (37)."

The slaves, who were at the bottom of the social scale, were either born unfree or lost their freedom through capture in war, bankruptcy or crime. These thralls were of no account and could be bought and sold at their owner's whim. They were employed as household servants or farmhands. The great mass of the people were karls, or free yeomen farmers, protected by the laws. They played some part in local government. This class included the craftsmen, soldiers and some of the merchants. The chieftains formed the smallest and most powerful class. They were warriors who collected together small armies and dominated the areas where they lived. There were some kings, but their authority was uncertain.

Women

Viking women were allowed far more freedom than their contemporaries in other European countries. Although their fathers usually arranged their marriages, some girls were allowed to choose their own husbands: "A maiden who is an heiress may marry whoever she likes when she is fifteen winters old with the advice of her closest and wisest relatives (38)."

Moreover, they could keep their lands after marriage: "A wealthy Icelander proposed marriage to the daughter of a rich man when she was fifteen summers old. She accepted him, but her father pointed out that she was of higher rank than her suitor. He took this well and replied that he wanted to marry the girl not her property. It was agreed that when they were married, the girl should control their property and own half of it (39)."

Marriage

A marriage was a great occasion and was marked by the gathering together of all the families related to the couple and the exchange of presents: "When Heidrek married Herborg, their wedding feast was the greatest the land had ever seen; it lasted for a month. When it came to an end, the chiefs were given presents of silver to take away with them and the father gave his daughter a rich dowry of gold and silver and many other costly things (40)."

Divorces were easy to arrange. Men could separate from their wives if they were bad housekeepers, childless or unfaithful, and women could leave their husbands if they were cruel, bankrupt or unfaithful. If a woman wanted a divorce and her husband refused to give her one, she could shame him into agreeing by parading around the district in trousers: "Thord declared himself divorced from Ard, because she wore trousers like a man (41)."

The Oseberg tapestry, showing fashionable Viking clothing

Before a chief went raiding, he called his household together and publicly handed over his keys to his wife. She gave all the orders while he was away: "Thorbjorg was a highly accomplished woman and very wise. She ruled the district and settled everything while Vermund, her husband, was away from home (42)."

The women looked after the cattle and made butter and cheese, ran the house and cooked the food. In addition, they spent much of their time spinning, weaving and embroidering: "She spent her time in the bower with her maidens embroidering in gold thread a

great tapestry depicting the deeds of Sigurd (43)." Lastly, they were expected to wash and delouse their husband's hair, and to pull off his clothes when he went to bed.

Babies

When a baby was born, it was laid on the floor until the father picked it up and wrapped it in the folds of his cloak. From its appearance, the father believed he could judge its future temperament, physique and luck in war. If the infant was deformed or ill-omened, it was exposed and left to die. One Viking law said: "Every child that is born into this world shall be brought up, carried to church and baptised except those that are deformed in any way. These shall be taken down to the beach and burned where neither men nor cattle go (44)."

Learning to survive

At an early age children were taught the basic skills they would need in life. The girls learned to sew and cook, milk the cows and make butter and cheese, and to spin and weave. They were taught to hoe and weed the fields, to ride and swim and to handle weapons so that they could defend themselves. If they wanted to marry well, they had to be able to sing, play an instrument and make conversation.

Idrottir

Boys learned to ride and swim, hunt and fish, forge iron and tan leather as well as how to handle weapons. By the time they were eleven or twelve, they started mastering the Idrottir, the skills of an educated man. Harald Hardradi said (45):

There are nine skills known to me—
At the chessboard I am skilful,
Runic writing I know well,
Books I like, with tools am handy,
good with snowshoes, rowing and shooting,
And expert with harp and verses.

The aim of this training was to make every boy a hero.

Runes

Early in their history, the Scandinavians had developed a runic alphabet. The runes were both magic symbols and letters. They were cut with a knife or chisel into wood or stone so that there are few curved lines:

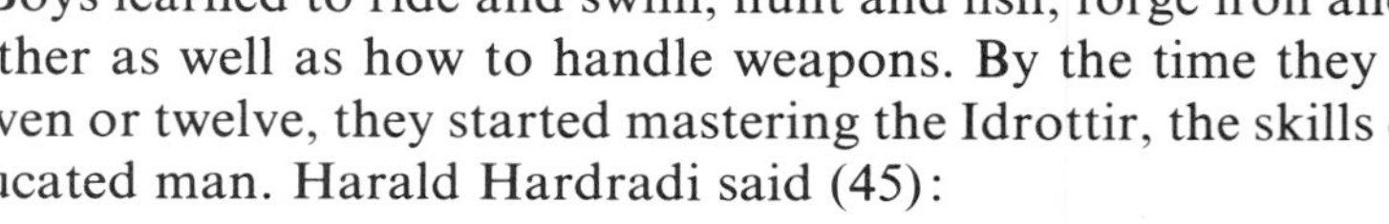

The Vikings set up runic monuments to the dead which sometimes give short histories of ordinary families, like this one (46):

The good farmer Gulle had five sons:
Asmund, the Brave fell at Fyris,
Assur died out East in Greece,
Halfdan was slain in a duel,
Kare died at Dundee and Boe is dead too.

Or this one (47):

Tola had this stone raised for his son Harald,
Ingvar's brother.
They went away on manly pursuits in search of gold
and in the East they provided the eagles with food.
They died in Sarkland [*the land of the Arabs*].

And finally, a wife's lament for her dead husband (48):

Tonne raised this stone over her husband Bram.
He was the best of landowners and the most generous.

Runic monument with inscription

Viking chess pieces, carved from walrus ivory

Sports In manhood, the Vikings continued to enjoy sports and games of all kinds. They played chess and draughts, sang ballads and told stories, swam, skiied and fenced. Falconry was a favourite pastime. They loved to train fierce birds of prey—falcons, hawks and eagles—to hunt wild birds and animals. One writer described how "the men walked into the king's hall with their hawks perched upon their shoulders, a splendid sight (49)."

Another told how. "One day, King Olaf rode out early with his hawks and dogs. When they loosed the hawks, the king's killed two woodcocks in one flight. He flew forward again and killed three more. The dogs followed them and caught every bird that fell to the ground (50)." The Vikings were so fond of peacocks that one warrior had his buried with him.

Dogs Dogs were their constant companions. Many stories were told about them: "When King Olaf was in Ireland, he went on a coastal raid. As his men needed provisions, some of them went ashore and drove off a large number of cattle and collected them on the beach. Soon afterwards a farmer arrived and asked Olaf to let him have his cattle back. Olaf agreed on condition that he could pick them out of the herd without delaying the drive. The farmer sent his sheep dog into the herd and in a few minutes, he had selected and cut out exactly the right number of cows bearing the farmer's brand. The Vikings had to admit that the dog had succeeded and thought him wonderfully wise. King Olaf asked the farmer if he would let him have the dog. 'Willingly,' answered the farmer. Olaf gave him a gold ring and promised to be his friend. The dog's name was Vigi. He was the best of dogs and Olaf owned him for a long time (51)."

A scale of awards was worked out to compensate owners for the loss of their dogs: "If a man kills a lapdog, he must pay twelve aurar; six aurar are to be paid for a greyhound; four aurar for a hunting dog or a sheep dog; and one aurar for a guard dog (52)." (An aurar was a Viking coin.) Even the Vikings had a soft spot for pet dogs, it seems.

Horses

Nonetheless, the Vikings loved their horses best of all. Their appearance is often described in the sagas: "Hrafn (the Raven) was as black as midnight and had hoofs as bright as stars. Slongvir (the Flinging One) was the colour of dandelions and was without equal (53)."

Their owners decked them out in every way possible: "Stein was so haughty that he had his horse shod with gold and had his hooves ornamented (54)."

Their affection did not stop them enjoying the cruel sport of horsefighting: "Thorstein and Thord arranged a fight between two young stallions. When they were brought together, Thord's did not want to fight so Thord struck Thorstein's stallion on the jaw with his cudgel. When Thorstein realised what he was up to, he hit Thord's stallion so hard that it ran away and all the men in the audience shouted with excitement. Then, Thord struck Thorstein on the forehead with such force that his flesh was torn and fell down over his eye (55)."

The Vikings enjoyed wrestling, swimming, running, jumping, balancing, climbing, racing on snow-shoes and playing ball games. Their competitive spirit often led to fights or brutal horseplay: "One fine day, many of the men from the longship and the merchant vessel went swimming. An Icelander amused himself by ducking all those who were weaker swimmers than himself. When King

Sigurd saw what he was doing, he threw off his clothes and dived into the water. He swam up to the Icelander, pushed him under the water and held him there. One of the King's friends swam to him and said, 'Don't drown the man, Lord; all can see that you are a far better swimmer than him.' The King let him go and swam back to the longship (56)."

Law

Strong laws were needed to control such violent men. They were jealous of their good name, and regarded "Gossip as the worst crime. The tongue that hurts most should be the most heavily punished (57)." These proud, quick-tempered men were only too ready to take offence; blows were often exchanged and people killed. This could lead to a blood feud: "There is an evil custom in this land of Norway that when a man has been killed, his kinsmen attack whoever is considered to be the most important member of the murderer's family even though the killing may have been without his knowledge or against his wishes. These people refuse to avenge themselves upon the murderer even though this could be easily done (58)."

A quarrel started in this way could continue from generation to generation and poison the life of whole communities. Unfortunately, the Viking *Things* (law courts) could do little to stop these feuds unless the local people were prepared to enforce their judgements.

Trial by battle

Trial by battle was one way to settle the issue: "If two Russian Vikings quarrel, they appear before their prince and argue their case in front of him. If they accept his judgement that is an end of the matter, but if they question his decision, he tells them to settle their dispute with their swords. The duel takes place in the presence of the friends of the two men who stand watching with drawn swords in their hands to see fair play. The man who gets the upper hand is the one who wins the case according to the rules (59)."

Weregild

Another solution was the payment of compensation or *Weregild.* Complicated tables of fines were drawn up covering every conceivable kind of injury to man or beast, for example: "When a man wounds another, he shall indemnify him at the rate of one eyrir for every muscle cut, one eyrir for every broken bone, one eyrir for every cut that bleeds and four aurar for every wound in vital parts (60)." (An eyrir was a Viking coin.)

Insurance

There were many sensible laws which helped ordinary people in distress. For example, if a farmer lost more than half his cattle through disease, he could claim up to half of their value from the rest of the community. Similarly, a man whose house had been burned down could apply for compensation for any three rooms and their contents.

Thus, it can be seen that Viking society was mostly well ordered, and that the level of their material culture was high. Contrary to general belief, they were not uncontrolled barbarians. As they said, "Cattle die, kinsfolk die and we ourselves die. One thing lives on—a man's reputation (61)."

3 *Gods and Graves*

Valhalla

AT THE BEGINNING of the Viking period, the peoples of Scandinavia were heathens who worshipped many gods. They believed that these gods lived in a great walled city called Asgard which contained Valhalla, the hall of the dead where warriors slain in battle feasted and sported for ever more: "Every day, after dressing, they put on their armour and go out into the enclosure where they fight and slay each other; this is their game. At dinner time, they ride home to Valhalla and sit down to eat and drink (62)." The hall had 640 doors, its rafters were huge shining spears and its tiles were gleaming golden shields.

The world of the gods was connected to earth, or Midgard, by a rainbow bridge called Bifrost. The earth was surrounded by a deep ocean filled with monsters. Beyond the ocean lay the land of Utgard, where the evil Frost Giants lived with whom the gods continually fought.

Niflheim

Beneath these worlds lay Niflheim. This was a land of mists, ice and snow to which the souls of all Vikings unfortunate enough to die in their beds were condemned. It is said that dying men pleaded with their friends and relations to kill them so that they might escape the horrors and boredom of this hell.

Odin

The greatest of the gods was Odin who was mysterious and dangerous: "Odin could change his shape: he was a bird, a beast, a fish or a serpent in the twinkling of an eye. Moreover, he could extinguish a fire, calm the seas and turn the winds in whatever direction he pleased by saying a few words. He had a ship called Skidbladir on which he crossed the seas and which could be folded up like cloth. He had two Ravens called Hugin and Munin which

Left Odin, the greatest of Viking gods, with his ravens, Hugin and Munin. A reconstruction

he taught to speak; they flew far and wide over the world and told him what they saw. In this way he became very wise (63)."

Sometimes Odin was seen, one-eyed and terrible, racing across the clouds on his eight-legged horse, Sleipner, dressed in a broad brimmed hat and a flowing cloak. Loping along on either side of him were his wolves Geri and Freki. He was married to Frigga and all the rest of the gods were descended from them, so that Odin was known as the Allfather. He was feared by the ordinary people and was worshipped solely by princes, poets and sorcerers.

Thor

The most popular god was the huge, red-bearded Thor who was not very clever but quick tempered and full of laughter: "Thor is the foremost and strongest of all gods and men. He owns two goats and a chariot which only they can draw. He possesses three very valuable things: his stone hammer, Mjolnir, his belt which doubles his strength, and his iron gloves without which he cannot hold his hammer (64)." When he dashed across the sky, the wheels of Thor's chariot rumbled and struck sparks from the floor of heaven causing thunder and lightning.

Frey

Frey was the god of love and marriage: "Frey was beautiful in looks, and mighty. He rules the rain and the sunshine, and has power over all that grows in the ground. It is well to make vows to him for good seasons and peace. He also controls men's fortunes in property (65)." Each autumn, the peasants drove carts bearing wooden idols of Frey from farm to farm, to prepare for the new season's planting.

A Viking temple

A monk called Adam of Bremen told of how these gods were worshipped in Sweden in the eleventh century: "The Swedes have a very famous temple at Uppsala, not far from the city of Birka. It lies in a great plain surrounded by mountains. Visitors can see it a long way off as its roof is covered with sheets of gold. In this temple, the people worship three gold encrusted idols—Thor, the mightiest of their gods, has his throne in the middle of the chamber while Odin and Frey have theirs on either side of him. They say that Thor is the ruler of the air and sky—the thunder and lightning, the winds and rain and the sunshine are his—as well as being the protector of crops. Odin is the god of war and fills men with courage to fight their enemies. Frey brings peace and pleasure to mankind. Sometimes, the people worship heroes whom they have made into gods

Statue of Loki, an evil Viking god

because of their great deeds.

"Priests are appointed to offer sacrifices to all their gods. When sickness or famine threatens, they pour out libations of wine to Thor; when they think about waging war, they make a sacrifice to Odin; and when they celebrate marriages, they offer gifts to Frey.

"Every nine years, they hold a great feast in Uppsala which all must attend. During the ceremony, nine males of every kind of living creature are slaughtered to please the gods. Dogs and horses hang side by side with human beings. A Christian told me that he had seen as many as seventy-two bodies hanging there side by side.

Prayers

"Near the temple stands a huge tree which bears green leaves all the year round. There is also a spring where the heathens make sacrifices. A man is lowered down into the spring, and if he does not

A Viking saga carved on rock

reappear that is a sign that the people's prayers will be granted (66)."

An Arab traveller called Ibn Fadlan spoke of the religious practices of the Vikings he met on a visit to Russia: "On beaching their ships on the banks of the river Volga, each Viking goes ashore carrying meat, onions, milk and beer. He takes these to a shrine containing a wooden idol with a face like a man's which is surrounded by smaller figures and a row of wooden stakes. The man throws himself on his face before the idol and says, 'O Lord, I have come from distant parts with so many slave girls and so many furs (and he lists all the trade goods he has brought with him). I offer these gifts to you.' Then, he lays his presents before it and continues, 'Please send me a rich merchant with plenty of money who will easily agree to my terms.'

"If business is slack, he returns to the idol and offers some more gifts. If trade remains bad, he turns to the smaller idols and begs their help. If his prayers are answered and trade picks up, he says, 'My Lord has satisfied my needs, now it is my duty to repay him.' Then, he sacrifices some goats and cattle: some of the meat he gives to the poor, the rest he places before the idols, large and small; the heads of the slaughtered animals are stuck on the poles behind the idols. Of course, as soon as it is dark, the dogs come and eat the lot but the happy trader says, 'My Lord is pleased with me and has eaten my offerings.' (67)"

Superstition

The Vikings also believed in and feared dwarfs, trolls, elves and the spirits of the dead. They thought that some spirits that looked like little old men with pointed hoods on their heads lived in the houses. If fed with bowls of milk and scraps, they might be set to work chopping wood, washing the dishes and helping around the house. But if they were neglected or upset, they created havoc—breaking valuable plates and cooking vessels and causing the women to cut, bruise and scald themselves. To protect themselves, the Vikings wore lucky charms—little figures of the gods made out of ivory and precious metals or tiny hammers (symbols of Thor)—on chains around their necks.

Soothsaying

They believed in black and white magic and thought that some people, soothsayers, could see into the future. A soothsayer is described in Erik the Red's Saga: "Thorkell invited a wise woman to his house and carried out all the special preparations required by custom; he had a high seat set out with a cushion stuffed with chicken's feathers. As soon as she arrived, she was given all the things she needed for her magic. She asked for the help of the women who knew the spells known as the Song of the Warlock.

"Then, the women formed themselves into a circle around the high seat, while one of them sang the spells so beautifully that all present said they had never heard singing like it. The wise woman thanked her and said, 'There are many spirits present and many things are revealed to me that I did not know before.' Then everyone went up to her in turn, and asked her whatever they wanted to know. She answered them all, and only a few things did not turn out as she predicted (68)."

Burials

When a man died, he was buried with all the things he would need in the next life. The best accounts of Viking burials were written by the Arabs. This description is by Ibn Rustah: "When a great man dies amongst the Rus [the Vikings in Russia], they make a grave like a large house and place him in it. His clothes, his arm-rings, some coins, large quantities of food and bowls of drink are put in with him. They also lay his favourite wife in the grave with him while she is still alive. Then, the mouth of the grave is blocked up and she dies there (69)."

Even more spectacular is Ibn Fadlan's account of the burial of a Rus chieftain: "One day, I heard that one of their great men had died. They laid him in the grave and covered him up for ten days while they finished cutting and sewing his burial clothes. Then, they asked his slave women, 'Which of you wants to die with him?' One of them answered, 'I do.' From that moment, she was placed in the care of two female servants who did everything for her, even washing her feet with their own hands. Every day, the doomed woman drank and sang as if she was looking forward to a joyous event (70)."

While this was going on, the men built a great funeral pyre and placed the chieftain's ship upon it. A tent was erected over the middle of the vessel where there was a couch covered with cushions and a mattress of Greek brocade:

"Then, an old woman whom they called the 'Angel of Death' came and arranged the cushions. She is in charge of the ceremony of preparing the corpse. She was a huge hag, fat and grim. They went down to the grave and lifted out the body. When they stripped it of its clothes, I saw that it had turned black with the intense cold. They dressed him in stockings, trousers, a tunic and a mantle with gold buttons; they placed a hat made of brocade and fur on his head. Then, they carried him to the tent on the ship, laid him on the mattress and propped him up with the cushions. Beer, fruit and sweet smelling plants were laid out all around the body in addition to bread, meat and onions (71)."

Various animals—horses, cows, hens and a dog—were sacrificed, cut to pieces and thrown into the ship. The slave girl performed various rites before she was taken to the ship and strangled as she lay beside her master.

Ibn Fadlan continues: "Now, the closest relative of the dead man appeared completely naked and picked up a piece of burning wood. With his face turned towards the crowd, he walked backwards to the ship and set fire to the pile of wood beneath it. Each person in the crowd threw a burning brand onto the pyre so that flames engulfed the whole ship, the man and the girl and everything in it. A strong wind began to blow so that the flames leapt higher and higher and the heat became more intense.

"As I stood watching, I heard one of the Rus say something to

Right Reconstruction of a Viking burial

my interpreter so I asked what he had said. He answered, 'He said, "You Arabs are fools." ' 'Why?' I asked. ' "Well, because you put those you love into the ground where insects and worms devour them whereas we burn them up so that they enter Paradise in a moment." '

"Within an hour, the ship, the pyre, the girl and her master were nothing but cinders and ash. On the spot where the ship had been, they built a round mound and placed a birch wood post in the middle upon which they wrote the names of the dead man and the King of the Rus. Then, they all went away (72)."

As we shall see in the next Chapter, the Vikings did not always burn these burial ships. This is fortunate for us, since they are one of the best sources of information about the Northmen.

4 The Longships

I'll mount my ocean steed
And o'er the hills I'll speed,
Forests and hills are not for me,
I love the moving sea (73).

THE VIKINGS loved ships. They carved them on stones, wrote poems about them and buried their great men in them. They gave them names like *Deer of the Sea*, *Wave Walker*, *Sea Bird* and *Raven of the Wind*.

The earliest ships

Tacitus, the Roman writer, described the Northern ships in 98 A.D.: "The Northern ships differ from the normal in having a prow at both ends. They do not rig sails. Their oars are loosely fitted and can be moved from one side to the other if necessary (74)." Masts and sails were not introduced until the eighth century.

Burial ships

The Viking longship was made entirely of oak. It was a long, narrow ship which drew so little water that it could be sailed up any river, beached upon almost any shore, and dragged overland for many miles when necessary. Three well preserved examples were found in Norway at Tune in 1867, Gokstad in 1880, and Oseberg in 1903. They had been buried beneath great mounds of clay which kept them dry and free from decay. Although incomplete, they have given archaeologists a wealth of information about life in the North.

Shipbuilding

When the Vikings built a ship, they had no plans or templates to guide them. Instead, they relied upon the skill of hand and eye to shape the timbers. Their tools were simple—axes, saws and adzes. The keel, or ship's backbone, was the first thing to be laid down; it projected down into the water giving the vessel a good hold on the sea and reducing sideways drift. The prow and stern pieces were carved out of great timbers and fitted to the keel.

Then, row upon row of planks were nailed onto the keel and each other, so that each row overlapped the one below it—clinker

The Gokstad ship

fashion—and were caulked with tarred rope. This planking was lashed to a framework of ribs and crossbeams which rested on the keel, but was not nailed to it, so that the hull was both strong and flexible. The top plank was bored through with holes to take the oars. The mast was fitted into a massive block of wood, called the mastfish, which rested on the keel; it could be raised and lowered with ease. The steering gear was very sophisticated: a huge oar was fixed to the starboard side by an axle of withies so that the helmsman

Typical prow of Viking longship

had only to push and pull on the tiller to steer the ship.

The Long Serpent

The best account of the building of a Viking ship is in Olaf Tryggvason's Saga: "King Olaf had a great vessel built which was bigger than any ship in the country. The length of the keel was seventy-four ells [yards]. Thorberg Skavhogg was in charge of its construction, while many others were engaged in the work cutting down trees, carting timber, cutting and shaping the parts of the ship, nailing and so on. The ship was long, broad and high-sided

Close-up of prow showing carved animal head

and made of strong timbers. While the planking was going on Thorberg was called away on business, and by the time he returned both sides had been finished. That evening, the King and Thorberg went to see how the ship looked. Everyone agreed they had never seen so large and beautiful a warship. Then, the King went back to town.

"Early next morning, Olaf decided to have another look at the ship but found all the carpenters standing around doing nothing. When he asked why, they told him that someone had hacked great lumps out of the planking during the night. When the King saw that they were telling the truth, he swore that he would kill the man responsible if he could lay hands on him. 'There will be a reward for anyone who can tell me who did it.' he added.

" 'I can tell you,' said Thorberg, 'I did it.'

" 'Then you will put right the damage or lose you life,' said the King.

"Thorberg set to work and thinned the planks until the axe marks disappeared. When the King saw what he had done, he realized that he had improved the ship. Thorberg remained chief shipwright until the vessel was finished.

"The King called this ship *The Long Serpent*. It had benches for thirty-four rowers and its dragon beak and arched tail were covered in gold. It was the finest and most costly ship ever built in Norway (75)."

The sails were square and made of wool, or a mixture of linen and wool. They were striped or chequered in red, blue, green and white. However, they did not depend entirely upon sails: in calms or narrow straits, they rowed the ship along with great oars, sixteen or seventeen feet long.

War ships

Some of the warships were very large: "Canute had a dragon ship of sixty rooms and Earl Hakon had another of forty rooms (76)." A "room" was the space allotted to each rowing bench which amounted to about a yard, so that Canute's ship must have been about 180 feet long and Earl Hakon's 120 feet.

The prows and sterns were carved into the shape of all kinds of animals and covered in gold, while the rest of the ship was painted: "The ships were so brilliantly painted that they dazzled the eyes of the beholder. To those that saw them a long way off, they seemed

Overleaf A fleet of Viking ships sweeps across the sea. Reconstruction

to be made of flames not wood. When the sun shone on them, one could see weapons glittering in one place and shields flashing in another. Their prows shone with silver and gold . . . Who could look upon those terrible lions in the brightness of their gold, those menacing men with their golden faces and those bulls threatening death with their golden horns, without fear (77)."

Shields

On special occasions, they fixed their shields along the sides of the ship so that each one overlapped its neighbour. Black and yellow shields were alternated in strict rotation to add to the effect. They made a brave show, as we can see in this extract from Njal's Saga: "At that moment, they looked out to sea and saw some ships come sweeping round the headland, rowing hard and making straight for them. War shields lined their gunwales and before the mast of the leading vessel stood a man with a magnificent head of hair who wore a silk tunic and a gilded helmet and carried a spear (78)." At sea, the shields had to be stowed under the benches as there were no permanent attachments for them.

Decks

The ships had two small decks, one at the bow and the other at the stern. These provided cover for food and goods, and served as strongpoints if the ship was boarded in battle. In harbour, large awnings were erected over the ship to shelter it from sun or rain: "When they came close to the islands, they saw a dragon head which shone like gold. They saw that there were twelve ships with the dragon, all covered with black tents. Light came from under the tents where the men sat drinking (79)."

The Knarr

So much for the warships. The ocean-going *knarr*, or merchant ship, was much more solidly built. It was shorter and broader in the beam, drew far more water, and had a higher freeboard. There were few oarholes as the ship depended almost entirely on its sail. The *knarr* was designed to carry heavy loads, and to cope with the Atlantic rollers. Until 1962, what little knowledge we had of these ships came from the sagas, but then archaeologists raised five wrecks from the bed of Roskilde Fjord in Denmark. They found two warships and three merchant vessels. One of the latter, a tubby ship some fifty feet in length, was identified as an "Ocean Striding Bison" in which the Vikings could have crossed the Atlantic to Iceland, Greenland and America. Such a ship is described in Egil's Saga: "Thorolf had a large seagoing ship which had been most carefully built and was painted almost everywhere above the waterline. It had a sail with blue and white stripes, and its rigging was very elaborate. He put dried fish, skins, tallow and furs on board and sent it westwards to England . . . When they arrived, they found a good market, loaded their ship with wheat and honey, wine and cloth and returned home in the autumn with fair winds (80)."

Provisions

On these voyages, the sailors needed plenty of food. They took casks of salted meat and smoked fish, sacks of grain, crocks of butter and cheese, sacks of apples and nuts, and barrels of beer and water. Whenever possible, they went ashore to cook some food; otherwise they had to make do with cold tack. Despite the lack of fresh fruit and vegetables at sea, the Vikings did not suffer from scurvy like so many of the sailors on the great voyages of discovery in the fifteenth and sixteenth centuries.

Life at sea

The ships must have been very crowded, and there was plenty of work to do. In rough weather, they had to bale out the ship: "When they were a long way out to sea, the waves began to rise fearfully high and there was such a snowstorm that the men in the bows and stern could not see each other, and the ship became so full of water that they had to bale the whole time (81)." In winter, they had to chip away the frozen spray which covered the ship in a coat of ice. During good weather, they checked and repaired the ship's rigging and gear and kept a lookout for landmarks and other ships.

The crew wore special clothes made out of animal skins, and slept in blankets or sleeping bags. One writer told how "they carried their sleeping bags from the ships to the huts on the shore (82)." Their personal belongings were kept in sea-chests which also served as rowing benches. They whiled away their leisure hours telling each other tales of the gods and famous Viking heroes. They played draughts and chess, using specially-bored games boards with pegged pieces, made so that the game could be played in rough weather.

Exploring the Atlantic

The Vikings were great navigators. They sailed across the Atlantic to Iceland, Greenland and America. How did this come about? The Atlantic discoveries were made by sailors who were blown off course during great storms (Chapter 8). Later, other captains followed their directions and established regular routes.

"The battle was fierce and bitter. Olaf's men threw grappling irons onto Swein's ships, but King Swein and his men escaped onto their other ships and drew back out of bowshot.

"Then, King Olov came alongside and attacked, but he suffered the same fate as the others, losing many men and several ships.

"But Earl Erik attacked the smallest ships on the end of Olaf's line and cleared them one by one and towed them away. Olaf's men jumped from these ships onto the larger ones. Then, the Danes and Swedes attacked from all sides. The battle was at its height and great numbers of men were slain. At last, all King Olaf's ships were captured except the *Long Serpent* which was packed with every man who could handle a weapon.

"Earl Erik laid his ship alongside the *Long Serpent* and the battle was continued with axe and sword. There was such a hail of arrows and spears that Olaf's men were unable to protect themselves against them. Many of them forgot that they were not fighting on land and rushed madly at the enemy, fell overboard and were drowned.

"King Olaf stood on the gangway of the *Long Serpent* shooting at the enemy with bow and arrow and hurling spears from both hands at once. In spite of this desperate defence, the centre of the *Serpent* was so thinned of men that Earl Erik was able to board her. So many of the Earl's men followed him that the King's crew was forced to jump overboard, where they were killed by the Earl's men in small boats.

"At the end, King Olaf himself leapt into the water. They tried to seize him, but the King raised his shield above his head and sank for ever beneath the waves (84)."

5 The Vikings in England

The first raid

ON A QUIET DAY in 793, a band of Viking sea-robbers attacked and destroyed the monastery on the holy island of Lindisfarne. This shocked all civilized people, like Alcuin, an English scholar at the court of Charles the Great who wrote: "Lo, for nearly 350 years we and our forefathers have inhabited this most lovely land, and never before has such terror appeared in Britain as we have now suffered from the pagan race; nor was it thought that such an attack could have been made from the sea (85)."

This was the first blow in a struggle between the Saxons and the Vikings which lasted until the overthrow of King Harold's Saxons at Hastings in 1066. The England they attacked was divided into no less than seven kingdoms whose peoples were continually quarrelling and fighting.

Mounting pressure

For forty years there was peace, and then the Vikings took advantage of the situation. In fact, from 835 onwards, hardly a year went by without a Viking raid being reported in the *Anglo-Saxon Chronicle* (a history of England started in the reign of Alfred the Great and continued down to the Norman Conquest and a little beyond). In 851 the Vikings wintered in England for the first time, and in 865 they forced the English to pay tribute or *Danegeld* for the first time. Then, in 867, the whole nature of the war changed when the three famous sons of Ragnar Hairy-Breeches*—Ivar the Boneless, Ubbi, and Halfdan—landed in East Anglia, marched across country and seized York, and then began to settle in Northumbria.

Wessex

By 871 the Vikings had overrun the North and the Midlands, and were ready to invade the last and most powerful of the Saxon

*See Chapter 6.

kingdoms, Wessex. Here, they were opposed by a 22-year-old prince called Alfred: "While King Ethelred [Alfred's elder brother] was still at his prayers, the Vikings arrived at Ashdown. Although he was only second-in-command, Alfred led the Saxons against their enemies with the courage of a wild boar and defeated them (86)."

Alfred the Great

Later, that year, Ethelred died and Alfred became King. Within a month, he was defeated by the Vikings at the battle of Wilton and forced by the exhaustion of his men to buy off his enemies. The Viking army divided in two. One half under Halfdan went north where they "shared out the land of the Northumbrians and started to plough and grow their own food (87)." The other half under Guthrum settled in Cambridge and waited for another chance to invade Wessex.

The navy

Meanwhile, a small Viking fleet sailing off the south coast received an unpleasant surprise: "875. King Alfred went out to sea with a naval force and fought against seven ships, capturing one and putting the rest to flight (88)." For the first time, the Vikings were challenged at sea. The King was quick to follow up his success: "877. King Alfred ordered that boats and longships should be built throughout the kingdom to fight the Vikings at sea. He put expert seamen on these ships to guard the sea approaches (89)."

The attack

While Alfred was busying himself with the fleet, Guthrum struck south: "878. In mid winter, the enemy went secretly to Chippenham. It occupied the land of the West Saxons and settled there. They drove a great part of the people overseas and conquered most of the others. All the people submitted to them, except King Alfred. With great difficulty he travelled through the woods and hidden places in the marshes . . . Afterwards, King Alfred with a small force made a stronghold at Athelney (90)."

Athelney

Alfred led many raids from this fort in the marshes and may even have acted as a spy: "While Alfred was in Athelney, he wished to find out the plans of the Viking army, so he disguised himself to look like a wandering minstrel and went boldly into their camp. He was able to get right into the innermost place where the Viking leaders were holding a council of war. There, playing his harp in a dark corner, he listened and looked as hard as he could and found out all their secret plans. He stayed in the camp several days until he was satisfied that he knew everything. Then, he stole back to Athelney, gathered together all his leaders and explained to them how easily they could beat the Vikings (91)."

Be that as it may, in the seventh week after Easter Alfred came out of hiding, and "rode to Egbert's stone east of Selwood where he met all the people of Somerset, Wiltshire and Hampshire, and they rejoiced to see him. And then after one night, he went to Iley and after another night to Edington, and there fought against the whole Viking army and put it to flight (92)."

Battle of Edington

The Saxons chased the Vikings back to Chippenham where Alfred remained for a fortnight working out the terms of a peace treaty. Guthrum handed over hostages and "swore great oaths" that he would leave the kingdom of Wessex. Three weeks later, Alfred enjoyed his greatest triumph: "King Guthrum with thirty of the men who were the most important in his army came to Aller which is near Athelney, and the King stood sponsor to him at his baptism (93)."

Danelaw

After the Treaty of Chippenham was made, Guthrum withdrew

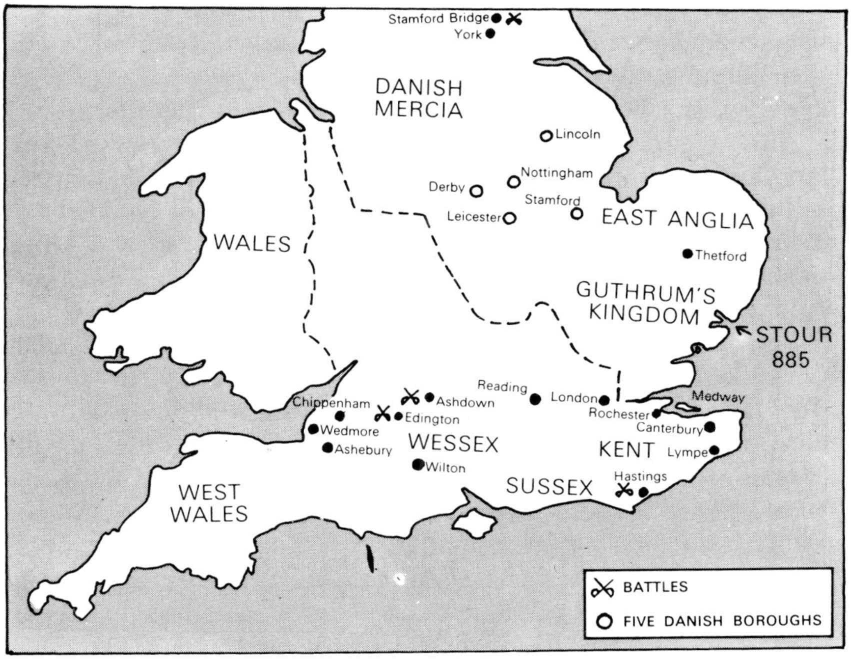

The England of Alfred the Great

to the "Danelaw." This was a territory which included East Anglia and the Five Boroughs of Derby, Stamford, Leicester, Lincoln and Nottingham. There is still plenty of evidence of the Viking settlement in these areas. For example, all place names ending in -thorpe (a village), -thwaite (a meadow) and -by (a farm or village) are Scandinavian in origin. When Domesday Book*was analysed, it was found that in the East Riding of Yorkshire, 40 per cent of the recorded place-names were Scandinavian; in the North Riding, 38 per cent, and in the West Riding 13 to 19 per cent.

The attack renewed

Things were fairly quiet for seven years, and then a new army arrived from the continent: "885. They besieged the city of Rochester and built defences around themselves. Nevertheless, the English defended the city until King Alfred came up with his army. Then, the enemy abandoned their fortifications and horses and returned to their ships. That summer, they sailed back across the sea (94)."

Now, Alfred went onto the offensive, and "sent a fleet from Kent to East Anglia. As soon as they entered the mouth of the river Stour, they met sixteen Viking ships and fought with them. They killed all the men and seized their ships. When they turned homewards with their plunder, they encountered a large Viking fleet. They fought against them the same day but the Vikings were victorious (95)."

Although this particular attempt to carry the war into the Danelaw failed, Alfred made steady progress on land and occupied London in 886. By this time, all the English looked on Alfred as their leader. Once again, there was an easing of pressure and Alfred was able to look to his defences. Fortified towns, or *burhs*, were built, and the Saxon army or *fyrd* drilled.

The great army

Then, after seven years, the "Great Army" attacked: "892. The Great Army came back from the eastern kingdom [Germany] to Boulogne where they were provided with ships and crossed over the Channel at one attempt, horses and all. They sailed up the estuary of the Lympne with 250 ships . . . and rowed as far as the Weald where they stormed a fortress, which was only half made and contained only a few peasants (96)."

This must have been one of Alfred's *burhs*. In 893, the Vikings were brought to battle at Farnam, and defeated and stripped of all their booty. Unfortunately, the Vikings in the Danelaw chose this

*A register of the lands of England, compiled (1084–6) by order of William the Conqueror.

moment to send a fleet of a hundred ships south to the north coast of Devon, so that the Saxons had to march to the West Country: "893. They overtook the Viking army at Buttington on the bank of the Severn, and besieged it on every side. Then, after they had been encamped for many weeks, the besieged were oppressed by famine: they had eaten the greater part of their horses and the rest had died of starvation. They then came out against the men who were encamped on the east side of the river and fought against them, and the Christians had the victory (97)."

There was a "very great slaughter," but many escaped and reached Essex where they prepared for another campaign. After two more years of fierce fighting, the Great Army broke up and the *Anglo-Saxon Chronicle* reported triumphantly: "896. By the grace of God, the army had not on the whole afflicted the English people very greatly; they were much more seriously hurt by the death of cattle and men, and most of all by that of many of the King's best thegns [nobles] (98)."

Death of Alfred

Alfred died in October, 899. He had saved England from being completely overrun, but the Vikings were firmly established in the Danelaw. He was succeeded by Edward the Elder (899–925), an able and energetic King who reconquered the whole of the Danelaw south of the River Humber. The next King, Athelstan (925–940), who was also powerful. His court was acclaimed by the sagawriters.

Conquest of the Danelaw

Nevertheless, the Northumbrian Vikings were restive, and in 937 they joined forces with the Scots and Norwegian Vikings from Ireland. Athelstan inflicted such a devastating defeat upon them at the battle of Brunanburh that the *Anglo-Saxon Chronicle* bursts into heroic verse (99):

Battle of Brunanburh

Here
Althelstan
Of earls the lord
Rewarder of Heroes
And his brother also
Edmund Atheling
Elder of ancient race,
Slew in the fight,
With the edge of their swords
The foe at Brunanburh.

In spite of this sharp lesson, the Northumbrian Vikings continued to be a menace until their last King, Erik Bloodaxe, was driven out in 954, when Northumbria became an English earldom. While the kings of Wessex extended their power, the Norwegian Vikings from Ireland were settling in the north-west and adding their influence to that of the Danish Vikings in the north-east and Midlands.

Edgar the Peaceable (959–975), who was recognized as King of all England, lived on good terms with the Vikings. He respected their customs and way of life, as this decree of 962 shows: "It is my will that there should be in force among the Danes such good law as they can decide on; I have ever allowed them this and will allow it as long as my life lasts, because of the loyalty which you have always shown me (100)."

Ethelred the Unready

Ethelred the Unready or Counselless (978–1016), the son of Edgar, was a very different kind of man; the Vikings soon renewed their attacks. The chroniclers point out the source of England's troubles in the following passage: "All these disasters befell us through bad policy in that the Vikings were never offered tribute nor fought against in time; only after they had done us the greatest injury was truce and peace made with them (101)."

Battle of Maldon

Often, local Saxon leaders were left to deal with the invaders as best they could; this is what happened to brave Earl Brihtnoth. His stand at the Battle of Maldon (991) was the subject of a fine Anglo-Saxon poem: "The messenger of the Vikings stood on the river bank and called sternly, 'It is for you to send treasure quickly in return for peace. It is better for you to buy off an attack with tribute than to fight with men as fierce as we are.'

"Brihtnoth grasped his shield and shook his supple spear and made angry and resolute answer: 'Hear you, sea-rover, what this folk says. For tribute they will give you spears, poisoned point and ancient sword.'

"Then, the wolves of slaughter pressed forward; they did not fear the water, that Viking host. West over the Blackwater, over the gleaming water they came with their shields . . .

"The heathen wretches cut him [Brihtnoth] down, and both the warriors who stood near by . . . (102)."

Danegeld

Faced by this resolute foe, Ethelred paid tribute in return for peace. But this merely whetted the Vikings' appetite, so that they

Right Vikings burn and plunder Canterbury in England

came more and more frequently, demanding larger and larger danegelds: 16,000 pounds of silver in 991, 24,000 in 1002, 36,000 in 1007, 48,000 in 1012 and finally 72,000 in 1018.

Typical of this unhappy period is the year 999: "The Vikings came round into the Thames and up the Medway to Rochester. The men of Kent came against them and fought bravely. But alas, they too soon turned and fled leaving the Vikings holding the field. Then, they seized horses and rode wherever they pleased and plundered and destroyed almost the whole of Kent. Then the King and his council decided that they should be opposed by a fleet as well as an army. But when the ships were ready there was one delay after another. Whenever preparations should have been going forward, they were delayed allowing their enemies to build up their strength. Always the English retreated inland and the Vikings pursued them. In the end, neither the fleet nor the army came to anything (103)."

Massacre of St. Brice's Day

The most cunning and persistent of Ethelred's tormentors was Swein Forkbeard, King of Denmark. He harried England mercilessly, until in rage and despair Ethelred ordered that "all the Vikings who had sprung up in this island should be destroyed by a most just extermination (104)." This led to the Massacre of St. Brice's Day on 13th November, 1002. Among the victims was Swein's sister, Gunnhild. Her death made Swein Ethelred's deadly enemy and fired his determination to conquer England. From 1003 onward there was no pause in the attacks.

"London Bridge is broken down"

In 1009, a Norwegian Viking, Olaf the Stout, found his progress up the Thames barred by London Bridge. So: "Olaf had great mats of willow and pliable wood made, and placed them over his ships so that they reached down over the gunwales. Underneath, he had timbers set up so thick and high that there was room for the swinging of swords and the screen was strong enough to withstand stones.

"When the fleet was ready, they rowed up the river to the bridge. When they drew near, so many stones were hurled down upon them that nothing could protect them, neither helmets nor shields. And so the ships were damaged and many had to withdraw; but Olaf's ships rowed right up under the bridge and tied ropes around the piles which supported it. Then they rowed off downstream with all their might. The piles were shaken until they loosened. When the piles broke away, the bridge burst asunder and many men fell into the river, and all the others fled from the bridge (105)." (This is the origin of the old nursery rhyme, *London Bridge is Broken Down.*)

Swein's plans went well until Alphege, the Archbishop of Canterbury, was brutally murdered: "The Vikings became very angry with the Archbishop because he would not promise to pay them any money but forbade that any should be paid for him. They seized the Archbishop and pelted him with ox-heads. One of them hit him on the head with the back of his axe so that he sent his holy soul to God's kingdom (106)."

Some of the Vikings were so shocked that they changed sides and joined Ethelred. This forced Swein to come to England to lead his armies in person. Ethelred fled to Normandy where he married Emma, the Duke's sister. When Swein died in 1014, he was master of England.

Canute

Swein's place was taken by his second son, Canute the Great. Canute "was very tall and strong, and a very handsome man except that his nose was thin, somewhat crooked and prominent. He had a fair complexion with long fair hair. His eyes were finer and keener than any other man's. He was generous, a great warrior, very valiant and victorious, and a man of great luck in everything connected with power (107)."

The Viking empire

Canute proved to be a strong and subtle ruler. He made his peace with the Duke of Normandy by marrying Emma, Ethelred's widow. He wooed the Christian Church and went on a well-publicized pilgrimage to Rome (1027). He added Norway to his empire by defeating and killing St. Olaf at the Battle of Stiklarstadir (1028). In all he ruled England, Norway, Denmark, Iceland and the Orkney and Shetland Islands.

While he reigned, Viking and Saxon lived happily together; but when he died everything changed. His son, Harthacnut, died unexpectedly as he stood drinking at a wedding feast (1042) and the rivals for the succession fell to fighting among themselves. While this was going on, the English elected as their King the only surviving son of Ethelred, Edward the Confessor (1042–1066).

Harald Hardradi

The Vikings made one more attempt to conquer England when Edward died childless. This time their leader was Harald Hardradi, "the Thunderbolt of the North": "He was a handsome and majestic looking man with auburn hair, beard, and long moustaches. One of his eyes was a little higher than the other. He was well formed with long arms and legs. He measured three ells in height (108)."

In September, 1066, Harald Hardradi swooped down on the Yorkshire coast, landed a large army, and defeated the Northern

King Canute and Queen Emma

Earls. Meanwhile, the English elected Harold Godwinson King and he marched north to deal with the invaders. The two armies met at the famous battle of Stamford Bridge on 25th September:

Battle of Stamford Bridge

"On Monday, after breakfast, King Harald Hardradi ordered his men to disembark and form up. The weather was exceptionally good with warm sunshine so that the Vikings left their coats of mail behind and took only their helmets, shields, spears and swords. A few of them had bows and arrows as well.

"As they drew near York, they saw a large force riding towards them [no English source mentions cavalry so this is probably an invention]. The horses' hooves stirred up a cloud of dust, but beneath it they could see the gleam of beautiful shields and shining coats of mail. The closer the army came, the larger it seemed and its weapons glistened like broken ice.

"King Harald took up position inside the circle of soldiers with his banner and personal bodyguard. Then, he rode around his army to inspect his men. He rode a black horse with a blaze which stumbled and threw him. The King jumped to his feet declaring, 'A fall means good luck will follow.'

Coronation of King Harold, last Saxon king of England

Battle of Hastings (1066), from the Bayeux Tapestry

"The English cavalry charged and the Norwegians met them without flinching. Time and again the English charged but had to fall back as they could make no headway. Then, the Norwegians thought that the English were half-hearted and charged the retreating cavalry. As soon as the shield ring was broken, the English rode down on them from every side and showered spears and arrows on them.

"When Harald saw this, he charged into the thickest of the fighting holding his sword with both hands. Neither helmets nor coats of mail could withstand his blows and everyone in his path gave way before him. At that moment, it looked as if the English were going to be defeated, but then King Harald Hardradi was struck in the throat by an arrow and mortally wounded (109)."

The *Anglo-Saxon Chronicle*'s account is more matter of fact: "A very stubborn battle was fought by both sides. Harald Hardradi

was slain and the remaining Norwegians fled while the English fiercely assailed their rear. Some reached their ships, some were drowned, others burned to death and others perished in various ways, so that there were few survivors . . . (110)."

Battle of Hastings

Three days later, an army made up of the descendants of the Vikings who had settled in Normandy arrived in England; they were led by Duke William. Harold hurriedly left the celebrations in honour of his victory at Stamford Bridge, and marched south. By the time he reached Hastings, he had "gathered together a great host and came to oppose William at the grey apple tree. William came upon him before his army was drawn up in battle order. Nevertheless, the King fought hard against him with those men who were willing to support him and there were heavy casualties on both sides. There King Harold was killed . . . (111)."

The Viking raids were over and England had new masters.

Moorish soldiers

6 The Vikings in Europe

THE VIKING ATTACKS on Europe followed a similar pattern to those on England. In the first half of the ninth century, they searched out their enemies' weaknesses by a series of hit-and-run raids up the great rivers. Later, the Viking fleets became larger, and bases were set up on islands near the coast so that the victims could be plundered systematically. By 900, the Vikings faced determined enemies everywhere, but still managed to carve out a new settlement for themselves in France.

Hit-and-run raids

The first stage of the attack on France is described in the *Annals of St. Bertin*:

"841. The Danish pirates from the Northern shores invaded the territory of Rouen and gave up the city, the monks and the lay people to death and captivity. They devastated all the monasteries and other places near the Seine and only left after they had been bought off with much silver.

"842. This time a fleet of Northmen entered Amiens at dawn. They plundered, captured and killed people of both sexes, and left no building standing that was not ransomed by its owners.

"843. The Northmen attacked the city of Nantes with a fleet of sixty-seven ships. Having killed the bishop and many of the priests and lay people, they pillaged the city and ravaged the lower parts of Aquitaine. Finally, on reaching the island of Noirmoutier, they built houses for the winter and settled down as if they meant to stay for ever.

"844. The Northmen advanced up the Garonne as far as Toulouse and plundered without opposition the land on every side. A group went off to Galicia [the north-west corner of Spain] (112)."

The Moors

In Galicia they came up against the Moslem Moors for the first time. An Arab historian described what happened: "The arrival of the Madjus [as the Moslems called the Vikings] struck terror into the hearts of the people, so that they fled and took refuge in the mountains. Nobody in western Spain dared to meet them in battle. Therefore the people of Cordoba and the surrounding districts were called to arms. Our leaders took up a position at Carmona, but dared not attack until the border forces arrived.

"As soon as they reached us, their chieftains asked if there was a place where they could lay in wait for the enemy without being seen. Our commander told them about the village of Quintos-Maafir to the south-east of Seville. They moved there in the middle of the night and set up an ambush. One of their men was sent with a bundle of faggots to keep watch from the tower of the village church.

Inflammable naptha shot from flame-throwers like this was used by the Moors against the Vikings in Spain

"At dawn, the sentry reported that 16,000 Madjus were marching on Moron. The Moslems let them pass, then attacked and cut them down. Then, our commanders entered Seville and joined forces with the governor who had been besieged by the Madjus in the citadel.

"When the Madjus saw the Moslem army coming, and heard of the disaster that befell their comrades at Moron, they took to their ships and abandoned the siege. While they were sailing up the river towards a castle, they met some of their countrymen, took them on board and began sailing down river. All along the route, the country people threw stones at them and cursed them. When they were a mile below Seville, the Madjus shouted to the people, 'Leave us alone if you want to ransom our prisoners of war.' Then, the people stopped throwing stones and were allowed to buy back the prisoners (113)."

The Moors proved to be formidable opponents. They took so many Vikings prisoner that there were not enough gallows in Seville to hang them all; so the local palm trees were used as well. The Emir, Abdul Rahman, sent 200 severed heads to his allies in North Africa as proof of the Vikings' failure. The Arab writer continues: "After this the Emir took measures to protect his country. He built an arsenal in Seville, ordered ships to be built and had sailors gathered on the coasts of Andalusia. He paid them high wages and equipped them with engines of war and naphtha [an inflammable substance that was fired from a primitive flame thrower] (114)."

Ragnar Hairy-Breeches

Undaunted by this drubbing, the Vikings attacked France even more fiercely next year. This time they were led by Ragnar Hairy-Breeches, the most famous of the early Viking leaders. The writer of the Annals of St. Bertin says:

"845. The Northmen sailed up the Seine in a hundred ships, ravaging here and there and arrived before Paris without opposition. King Charles the Bald intended to go against them but, seeing little chance of success, left them alone and bought off their attack with 7,000 pounds of silver (115)."

Ragnar hanged 111 prisoners on an island in the Seine in full view of the Frankish army to rub in his victory. Next year, the main attack was switched to Germany:

"846. Eurich, the King of the Northmen, sailed up the River Elbe with 600 ships against Lewis of Germany. The Saxons went forward to meet them, gave battle and with the help of Our Lord Jesus defeated them (116)."

And so with every year the number and range of raids increased until by the 860s the chronicler Ermentarius of Noirmoutier wailed: "The number of ships increases, the endless flood of Vikings never ceases to grow bigger. Everywhere Christ's people are the victims of massacre, burning and plunder. The Vikings overrun all that lies before them and none can withstand them (117)."

The great raid

One raid above all others deserves to be remembered, that of Bjorn Ironside and Hasting. They were driven from their base on

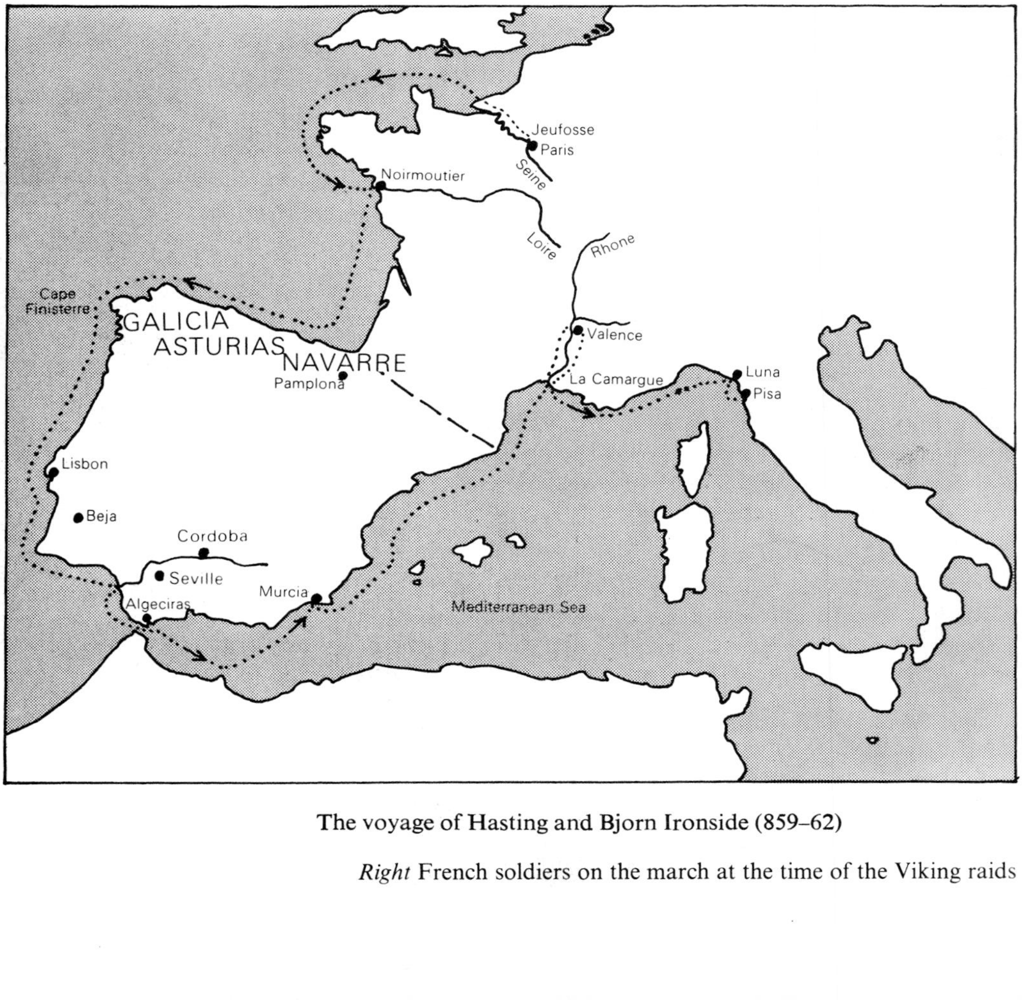

The voyage of Hasting and Bjorn Ironside (859–62)

Right French soldiers on the march at the time of the Viking raids

ET SYRIAM SOBAL · ET CONVERTIT
IOAB · ET PERCVSSIT EDOM IN VAL
LE SALINARVM · XII MILIA ·

the Island of Jeufosse in the Seine, and made for Spain. Ibn Adhari recorded: "In the year 959, the Madjus were seen again on the west coast, this time with sixty-two ships. They found it well guarded as Moslem ships patrolled the coast between France and Galicia. Two of their vessels were hunted down by our guardships and captured. They contained gold, silver, slaves and provisions. The other Madjus ships sailed along the coast to the mouth of the Guadalquivir. The Emir Mohammed ordered the army to meet them, but the Madjus left the rivermouth and sailed to Algeciras where they captured the town and burned down the grand mosque.

"Then, they crossed the sea to Africa and plundered the people of that country. After that, they returned to the coast of Spain and landed in the province Murcia. From there, they sailed to southern France and spent the winter on the island of La Camargue. They took many prisoners, stole a lot of money and made themselves masters of the city where they settled (118)."

In the spring, they made a short expedition up the River Rhône and captured the city of Valence. Then, they decided to sack Rome itself and sailed south until they sighted the large, white, and richly decorated city of Luna which they mistook for Rome:

"The wicked robber Hasting sailed to the city of Luna and hoped by a sudden attack to make himself master of it. But the citizens were terrified by the sight of such a large fleet, and took up arms and defended their walls with spear and shield. So great was their spirit that in spite of all his efforts Hasting could not seize the town by force, so he tried trickery instead.

"He sent his servants to the bishop and count of the city to tell them that he was suffering from a fatal illness and humbly requested to be allowed to end his days as a Christian. On hearing this, the bishop and count rejoiced greatly, and made peace with this enemy of peace. The Vikings were allowed to come and go as they pleased. At length, the wicked Hasting was carried to church and baptised and then carried back to his ship by his servants.

"It was no surprise to the Christians, therefore, to hear next day that he had died claiming the right to Christian burial in consecrated ground. Accordingly, the bishop and the count prepared to receive the body of the dead sea King. In the middle of the night, Hasting dressed in armour and laid down upon a bier, and ordered his followers to wear their coats of mail beneath their tunics.

"The next day, his sorrowing comrades carried him to church where the bishop in his holy vestments was ready to say the Mass for the Dead. When the Mass was over, they made ready to lay him in the grave but all the Vikings shouted, 'No!' Then, Hasting, that son of the Devil, sprang from the bier and put the bishop and the count to the sword and fell upon the people with wolvish rage. Neither old nor young were spared, the city was pillaged and its walls thrown down (119)."

In 861, the Vikings appeared off the Spanish coast again. Ibn Adhari continues the story: "When they returned to Spain the following year, they had already lost more than forty of their ships in a storm [an exaggeration] and when they joined battle with the Emir's fleet off the coast of Sidonia, they lost two more loaded down with great riches. The others got away (120)."

The survivors were not discouraged by this change in their fortunes. When they reached Navarre, they marched inland and captured Pamplona and its prince. They collected an immense ransom before sailing north once more. In 862, a third of the original fleet reached the Isle of Noirmoutier off the Loire with their loot and negro slaves.

Siege of Paris

Meanwhile, the King of France, Charles the Bald, tried to keep the Vikings out of his country by building barriers across the rivers. But this did not succeed, and he had to pay more and more Danegeld. On his death, another Charles, Charles the Fat, came to the throne and proved no stronger. In 885, a fleet of 700 ships carried "the Great Army" of 40,000 Vikings up the Seine. Their objective was the rich land of Burgundy in eastern France; but to reach it they had to pass Paris.

At this time, Paris was a small walled town on an island in the Seine; stout wooden bridges guarded by towers linked the city to both banks of the river. The Viking leader, Siegfried, wanted to avoid trouble and offered to spare the city if he was allowed to sail up the river unmolested. But, Jocelin, the Bishop of Paris, and Count Odo refused to agree, even though their garrison numbered a mere 200 men.

Abbo of Fleury left an eyewitness account of the ensuing siege: "The Vikings made three huge siege engines out of immense oak

Reconstruction showing Siegfried's Viking fleet besieging Paris (886)

trees which they bound together and mounted on sixteen wheels. A battering ram was rigged up inside each machine and covered by a high roof. They concealed as many as sixty men inside each one. The Vikings finished one, then another and were at work on a third when death came to them from the archers on the walls.

"During the night, the enemy took no rest, and not a moment of sleep. They sharpened and repaired their old weapons and made new ones . . . At dawn, those children of the Devil rushed from their camp towards the towers on the bridge. Thousands of lead balls from their slings fell like hail upon the city and powerful catapults were fired at the walls (121)."

Even these monstrous weapons failed to pierce the walls of Paris, so that the Vikings withdrew for a time. Then, suddenly, they attacked on 29th January, 886: "The fierce Viking, Siegfried, divided his army into three parts and arranged them in wedge formation. The largest part he directed against the tower and the other two he sent against the bridge in painted ships, thinking that if the bridge fell the tower would be his. The tower, reddened with blood, groaned under the blows it received . . . The ground was hidden from the sight of the defenders by the huge numbers of Northmen. Stones and arrows filled the air like swarms of bees . . . Loud cries were heard and everywhere there was the greatest fear. The Northmen banged their weapons together to make the battle more horrible. Then, they raised their painted shields above their heads and rushed to the base of the tower. There, they tried in vain to fill up the ditch and to create a breach with their battering rams, but the defenders poured flaming oil onto the siege engines and set them on fire (122)."

Infuriated by this spirited resistance, the Vikings tried to burn down the northern bridge: "Furious at being unable to bring their foe into the open, the Northmen took three ships, filled them with wood and set fire to them. A favourable wind bore the burning vessels towards the bridge but they lodged against its stone piers and burned away harmlessly. The defenders sallied forth and destroyed them (123)."

Once again, famine forced the Vikings to retire, but the Parisians rejoiced too soon, for they returned to the attack as soon as their bellies were full. Now, the weather struck the defenders a cruel blow: "Alas, during the silence of the night, the middle of the bridge fell in, carried away by the fury of the flood waters. At dawn, the cruel Vikings awoke, boarded their ships, crossed the Seine and surrounded that unhappy tower. At last, after a desperate struggle, the Vikings placed a wagon full of grain in front of its gates and

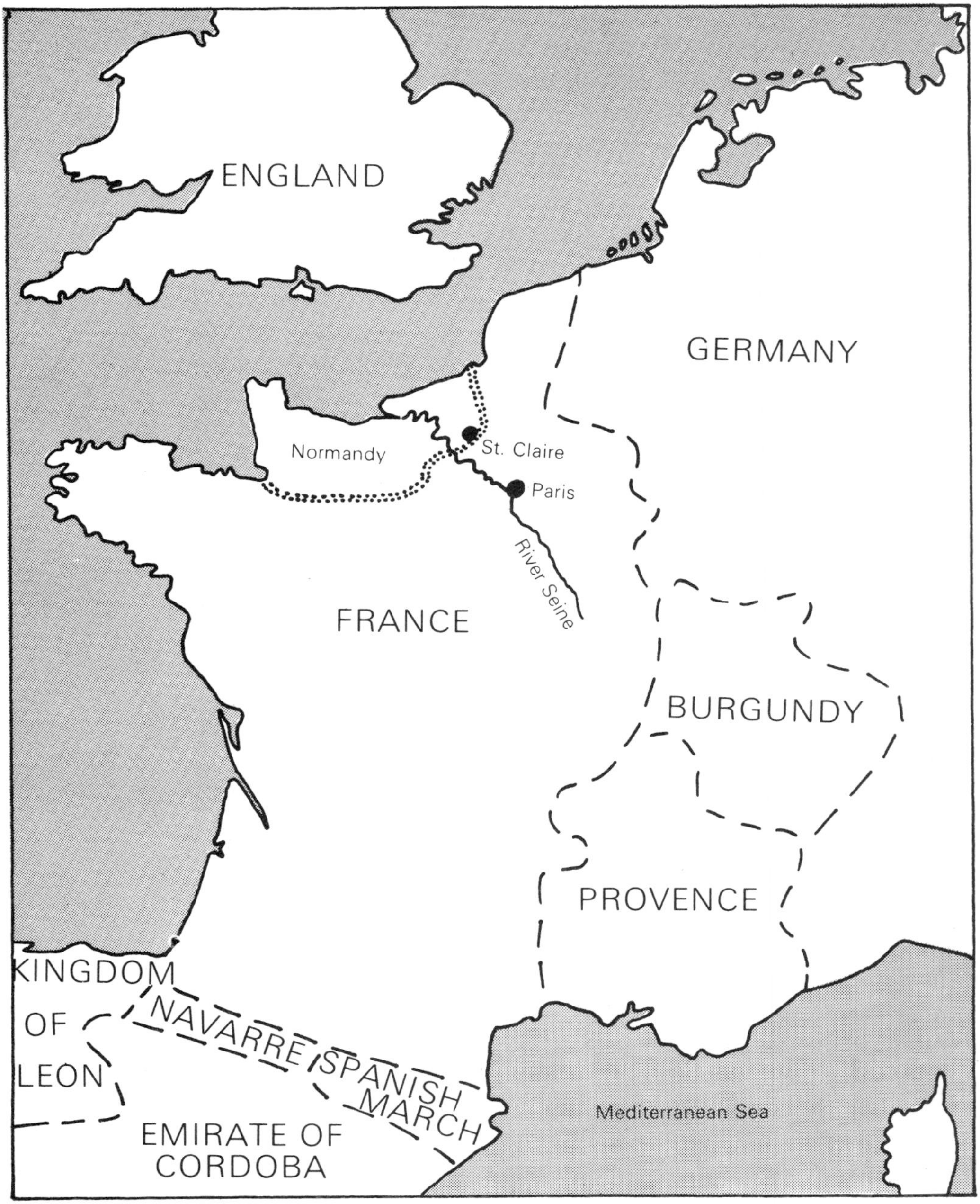

Rollo's Duchy of Normandy

set fire to it. Then, they withdrew and allowed the flames to do their work. Being without water, the tower was burned down and the garrison had to retire to the end of the bridge where they continued to fight until nightfall (124)."

Finally, the garrison was butchered. Part of the Viking fleet passed upstream while the rest continued the siege. At this moment, Charles the Fat appeared with a large army, so that Siegfried, who was sick of the whole affair, allowed himself to be bought off with a paltry sixty pounds of silver. However, many of the Vikings stayed, and another full scale assault was launched in August. But at long last Charles relieved the city. The Parisians expected the King to hurl himself upon the Vikings, but instead he gave them a free passage up the Seine and promised to pay them 700 pounds of silver.

Rollo and the founding of Normandy

As a result of this cowardice Charles was deposed and replaced by the brave defender of Paris, Count Odo. King Odo harried the Vikings to such good effect that the Great Army moved away in 893, and attacked England. Twenty years passed before a really powerful Viking army again invaded France. Its leader this time was Rollo, or Rolf: "He was so tall that no horse could carry him so he walked wherever he went and was named Rolf the Ganger (125)."

William of Jumierges described how the King, Charles the Simple, dealt with this crisis: "The King sent off Archbishop Franco and his envoy with all speed to Rollo to tell him that, if he would become a Christian, he would give him all the coastal lands from the River Epte to the borders of Brittany and his daughter Giselle in marriage. Rollo accepted these offers on the advice of his followers, stopped his plundering, and arranged a three months' truce with the King.

"At the appointed time, the King went to St. Claire on one side of the River Epte while Rollo appeared with his men on the other side. Then, messengers went backwards and forwards between them until by God's will peace was concluded.

"When the moment arrived for Rollo to be invested with the Duchy of Normandy, the bishops told him, 'When you receive the award, you must kneel and kiss the King's foot.' Rollo answered, 'I have never bowed my knees before any man, still less kissed his foot.' In the end he gave way to the pleadings of the Franks and ordered one of his followers to kiss the King's foot. The Northman bent down and seized the King's foot and stood up to kiss it throwing the King on his back amidst the roars of laughter of the common people (126)."

Nevertheless, Rollo proved to be a model subject. In 912, he was baptised and married Giselle. Then, he divided up his estates amongst his men who settled down to farm the land; hundreds of Scandinavian place names have survived in Normandy as they have in England. They usually end in "bec", "fleur", "beuf", "ham", "dalle" and "tot".

Rollo strengthened the defences of the towns and maintained law and order throughout the Duchy. He guarded his lands against other groups of Vikings and even helped to put down a rebellion led by the Duke of Burgundy and was rewarded for his loyalty with further grants of land. The Vikings inter-married with the Franks and quickly adopted their religion, language and customs so that there was little to distinguish the Normans from any other Frenchmen when they invaded England in 1066.

7 *The Vikings in Russia*

DURING THE NINTH CENTURY, the Swedish Vikings settled in Russia. The native people were tribes of Slavs who subsisted upon what they could grow—wheat, barley and millet—and what they could hunt and fish. The Slavs were constantly fighting one another and this, according to the chroniclers, led them to invite the Rus or Swedish Vikings into their land:

"They said to themselves, 'Let us find a prince who will rule over us according to the law.' So they sent messengers to the Rus and said, 'Our land is large and rich, but there is no order in it. Come and rule over us.' They chose three brothers and their kinfolk who migrated taking all the Rus with them. Rurik, the eldest brother, settled in Novgorod, Sineus, the second brother, in Byeloozero; and Truvor, the third, in Izborsk (127)."

The Rus

An Arab geographer called Ibn Rustah gave a vivid account of these Rus in the tenth century: "The Rus live on an island in a lake [probably Novgorod]. It is covered in undergrowth and woods and takes three days to walk round. It is very unhealthy and so marshy that the ground squelches under one's feet. They have a prince whom they call the Khaquan. The men from this island go out in their ships to raid the Slavs; they seize them and carry them off to the empires of the Khazars and Bulgars in the east where they sell them as slaves.

"They do not cultivate the land themselves but live on what they get from the Slavs. When a baby boy is born, his father walks up to him and throws down his sword saying, 'I won't have anything to leave to you when I die so you will have to get what you can for yourself with this sword.' They have no estates or villages or fields

and their only business is trading: they sell the pelts of sables, squirrels and other animals. They are paid for their goods in coins which they keep hidden in their belts. Their clothes are clean and the men decorate themselves with gold armbands. They treat their slaves well and wear splendid clothes as befits traders. They have many towns.

"The Rus honour their guests, and are kind to all strangers who ask them for shelter, and to anyone who is in trouble. They do not allow anyone to annoy their guests or do them any harm. If anyone dares to insult them or do them an injustice, they help and defend them.

"They have witchdoctors who are very powerful. They decide how many men, women and animals should be offered to their gods. When the victims have been chosen, the witchdoctor takes them and hangs them from poles until they are dead, saying, 'This is a sacrifice to the gods.'

"The Rus are full of courage in battle and once they attack an area, they continue fighting until they have destroyed it. They take the women prisoner and make the men slaves.

"They are well built, good looking and daring although they do not appear so on land. They always go on raids and expeditions by water, never by land (128)."

Dnieper trade route

Gradually, the Rus made their way overland and down the River Dnieper to the Black Sea where they made contact with the Byzantine Empire. Once the great city of Kiev had been established, trading expeditions went to Constantinople every year, as a Byzantine Emperor described: "The ships that come from northern Russia to Constantinople start from Novgorod which is the capital of the Prince of the Rus and from the cities of Smolensk, Teliutza, Chernigov and Busegrad. Boats from all these towns make their way down the river Dnieper and assemble at Kiev.

"During the winter, the Slavs cut down trees and hollow them out. When the spring comes and the ice melts, they carry them down to the lakes that empty into the Dnieper and float them down to Kiev where they sell them to the Rus. The Rus will only buy empty shells because they like to fit out the boats with the oars and row-locks and all the other tackle from their old vessels which they take to pieces.

Left Rurik, reputed to be founder of Russia

"In June, they sail down the river to Vitichev and wait there two or three days until all the boats have arrived, and then move off down river.

"After a time, they come to a set of rapids which bar their way. These are as wide as a polo ground and have dangerous rocks which stand out like islands—the water rushes up and over them and plunges down the other side with a terrifying roar. Therefore the Rus do not dare to sail between them, but lay their boats alongside the bank before this point and make most of the people disembark although the cargoes are left on board. They walk into the water naked, testing the river bottom with their feet so as not to stumble over stones. There are many men at the bows, amidships and in the stern thrusting the boats forward with poles. In this way, they edge their way past the rapids. Then, they pick up the rest of the crew and sail on (129)."

Using the same technique, they passed through a second and third set of rapids, but at the fourth a new danger appeared: "On this occasion, the Rus turn their boats' prows into the bank and run them aground. Then, they send out a company of guards into the surrounding countryside to watch for the Petchenegs, their enemies, who are always lurking in ambush for them. They unload the boats and march their slaves in chains across country for six miles. Then, the boats are lifted out of the water and half carried and half dragged overland. Once past the rapids, they put them back in the water, load them with cargo and sail off again (130)."

They passed through seven cataracts in all before stopping for a rest and to give thanks: "Finally, they reach an island named after St. Gregory where they land and offer sacrifices to their gods as there is a gigantic oak tree growing there. They offer up live cocks, make a circle by sticking their spears in the ground, and set out some of their bread and meat and a little of anything else they possess. They draw lots to determine the fate of the cocks—whether to slaughter them, eat them themselves or let them go free (131)."

Constantinople

At length, they reached the mouth of the Dnieper and sailed along the shores of the Black Sea to Constantinople; in this great Eastern city they obtained wines, silks and naval stores. They were deeply impressed by Constantinople—Miklegard, the Great City, they called it. Here is part of a description of the city written by an

Arab in the ninth century:

"The sea flanks Constantinople on the east and a plain that leads to Rome on the west. The Roman Gate is made of gold and has five statues on it in the form of elephants and a man holding their

The Land of the Rus

reins. The Imperial palace is near the church in the middle of the city. Beside it is the Hippodrome or race track. At the palace end of which are brass statues of horses, men, wild beasts—lions and the like. At the west end, there are two gates to which two golden chariots are driven; the charioteers are dressed in silk and drive their chariots at great speed—they start from the gates and race three times around the statues. The winner is awarded a golden necklace and is given a present of gold by the Emperor. All the people of Constantinople attend these races . . .

"The Imperial palace is surrounded by a wall that reaches the sea in the west. Through the entrance chamber, there is a courtyard with a curtained door to the palace. If you raise the curtain, you will see another huge courtyard inlaid with green marbles, its walls adorned with mosaics and paintings (132)."

Inside the palace, there were greater wonders still: "Before the Emperor's seat stood a tree made of gilded bronze whose branches were filled with birds of like metal who each sang the song of its own kind. The throne was so marvellously constructed that at one moment it would be close to the ground and at another it would rise into the air. It was of immense size and was guarded by bronze or wooden lions covered in gold, who beat the ground with their tails and roared dreadfully with great open mouths and quivering tongues (133)."

No wonder the Vikings were overawed. However, their feelings of awe soon changed to greed, and they made several attempts to plunder the city. In the early 860s, the first rulers of Kiev ravaged the shores of the Black Sea and reached Constantinople; but they were forced to withdraw by a terrible storm.

In 907, the Rus returned, led by Oleg, who had united Novgorod and Kiev: "He arrived before Constantinople with 2,000 ships, but the Greeks fortified the strait and put a boom across the Bosphorus. Oleg landed and ordered his men to beach their ships. They plundered the land around the city and killed many Greeks. Of the prisoners they captured, some were beheaded, some tortured, some shot, and some thrown into the sea.

"Then, Oleg ordered his men to make wheels and fix them onto the ships so that when there was a favourable wind, the sails were spread and they bore down on the city from the open country. When

Detail from a casket showing two Byzantine soldiers

the Greeks saw what was happening, they were afraid and sent messengers to Oleg imploring him not to destroy the city, and offering to pay whatever tribute he should demand (134)." Whatever the truth of this story, the Emperor certainly granted the Rus a favourable treaty in 912. Further attacks took place in 941 and 944 under Prince Igor, which resulted in another treaty.

The Volga route

However the River Dnieper was not the only Russian trade route. Many of the Rus went further afield to the upper waters of the Volga in eastern Russia. This area was ruled by the Khazars and the Bulgars, who let the Rus pass through their lands in return for a share of their profits. They crossed the Caspian Sea and carried their wares to Baghdad, the capital of the Arab Caliphate. There, they exchanged their furs, slaves, honey and wax for Persian glass, Chinese silks, Far Eastern spices and Arab silver. We can judge how important this trade route was by the fact that archaeologists

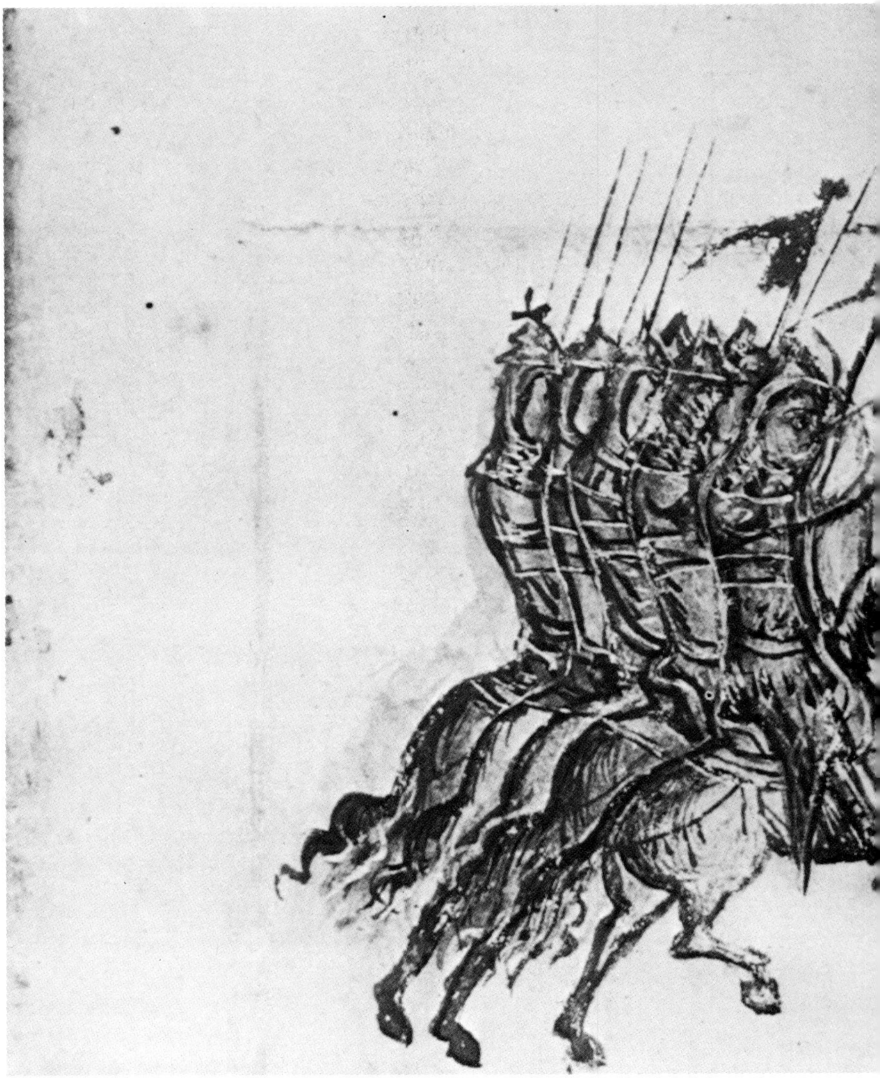

Bulgar soldiers

have unearthed in Scandinavia some 85,000 Arab coins compared with a mere 500 Byzantine coins.

Rus traders

An Arab diplomat called Ibn Fadlan wrote a vivid description of the Rus he met on a visit to the Bulgars in 922: "I saw the Rus

when they arrived on a trading expedition and camped on the banks of the River Volga. Never have I seen men with more perfectly developed bodies—they were as tall as date palms with blond hair and ruddy complexions. They wear neither tunics nor coats but have cloaks which cover one side of their bodies and leave one hand free. A man is never parted from his axe, sword and knife. Their swords are broad, flat and grooved like those of the Franks. Every man is tattooed from his finger nails to his neck with green trees and figures.

"Every woman wears a brooch on her breast made of iron, copper, silver or gold, depending upon the wealth of her man. A knife hangs from a ring on this brooch. She wears a number of gold or silver rings around her neck: when a man has made 10,000 dirhams, he buys his wife a neck ring, when he has 20,000 he gives her another and so on. A woman may have many rings. Their finest ornament is the green clay-pearl. They go to great trouble to obtain them. They buy a pearl for a dirham and when they have enough string them together to make necklaces for their women.

"When they arrive they build large wooden houses on the banks of the Volga. Ten or twenty people live in each house. Each Rus has a bench on which he sits and diverts himself with the pretty slave girls whom he has brought along to sell. He will make love with one of them while his comrades look on. Sometimes, it may happen that while they are all making love a merchant comes in to buy a girl from one of them. If he is making love with her, he will not let her go until he has finished with her.

"They are the filthiest of God's creatures: they do not wash their hands after going to the lavatory or after meals. They are as lousy as donkeys. They wash their hands and faces every day in incredibly dirty water. Every morning, a girl brings her master a large bowl of water in which he washes his hands, face and hair before blowing his nose and spitting into it. When he has finished the girl takes the bowl to the next man who repeats the process. In this way the bowl is passed around the entire household.

"When one of the Rus falls sick, they put him in a tent all by himself with some bread and water. While he is ill, they do not visit him or speak to him especially if he is a slave. If he gets better, he rejoins the others; if he dies, they burn him. But if a slave dies, they leave his body in the open so that the dogs and vultures can eat his flesh. If they catch a thief, they hang him in a tree and leave him there until the wind and weather have torn his body to shreds (135)."

After this, Ibn Fadlan described the burial of the Rus chieftain (p. 50). He continued: "It is usual for the king of the Rus to have a bodyguard of 400 loyal men who have sworn to die for him. Each soldier has a slave girl to wash him, wait on him and serve him and another to go to bed with. These 400 men sit below the royal throne on a large bejewelled platform which also contains forty girls of the royal harem. Everything is done for the king: if he wants to pass water, a basin is brought to him for that purpose. When he wants to go riding, they lead his horse right up to him so that he can mount, and when he returns he rides right up to the throne before dismounting. A deputy leads his armies in battle and holds audiences with his subjects (136)."

This account of the Volga Rus shows how much they were influenced by the customs of the eastern lands: their weapons, religious practices and burials remained the same, but their way of life and dress became oriental.

Raid on the Caspian

As in the case of the Byzantine Empire, the Rus' greed led them to attack and plunder the lands around the Caspian Sea in 912: "The Rus fleet of 500 ships, each containing no less than 100 warriors, reached the mouth of the River Don and asked the King of the Khazars for permission to sail down his river to the Caspian Sea and offered him a half share of all the plunder they expected to obtain. He agreed and the Rus entered the estuary, sailed up the Don as far as the Volga, and then sailed down that river past the city of Itil [which lay close to the modern city of Astrakhan] and into the Caspian.

"They looted far and wide, shedding blood, stealing people's goods and making their children prisoners. The local people were bewildered because they had never had to face enemies from this quarter before. When the Rus had had their fill of collecting booty and prisoners, they sent the King of the Khazars his share of the plunder and set out for home.

"When the Moslems heard what the Rus were doing, they approached the King of the Khazars and said, 'The Rus have invaded the lands of our Moslem brothers and have spilled their blood and made their wives and children prisoners. As our brothers cannot defend themselves, let us deal with the Rus.' The King could not refuse their request but sent off messengers to warn the Rus.

"The Moslems collected a large army of about 15,000 infantry and cavalry and marched along the banks of the Volga. When the Rus saw them, they left their ships and formed up in battle order. Then, the two armies fought together for three days and God gave the Moslems victory. Some of the Rus were put to the sword, some drowned, and about 5,000 escaped in their ships. About 30,000 dead were counted on the banks of the Volga (137)." The Rus attacked again in 943 but were decimated by dysentery and Moslem attacks.

Decline of the Rus

Gradually, the Rus declined in power. The Arab silver mines were exhausted and the Vikings found a new source in Germany; about 70,000 German coins have been found in Scandinavia dating from the late tenth and eleventh centuries. As we have seen, the Rus gradually absorbed the native cultures and lost their own characteristics. Although diminished in size and importance, the trade with Constantinople continued until the time of the Fourth Crusade (1202–1204).

The Swedish Vikings played a great part in founding modern Russia. It is only right that they should have given their name—Rus—to their adopted country.

8 Explorers of the Atlantic

The western movement

WHILE SOME VIKINGS were attacking Western Europe, others were exploring the unknown waters of the Atlantic and discovering new lands. The mysterious expanse of the Atlantic must have offered a great challenge to the skilled seamen living along the west coast of Norway.

Another more pressing motive for exploration was tyranny: "Owing to King Harald Fairhair's oppression, many people fled from Norway and settled in many uninhabited lands—the Hebrides, Dublin in Ireland, Caithness in Scotland, the Shetlands, France and the Faroes (138)."

Iceland

In about 860, the Vikings discovered Iceland: "Once upon a time, men—some say it was Naddod the Viking—set out from Norway bound for the Faroes but drifted into the Atlantic and found a large new island (139)." Several other explorers reconnoitred the island before a real attempt was made to found a colony, then:

"Two foster brothers, Hjorleif and Ingolf, sailed together until they sighted Iceland where they got separated. When Ingolf sighted Iceland, he cast the pillars of his seat* overboard and vowed that he would make his home wherever Thor thought fit to bring them ashore. Then, Ingolf landed and spent his first winter in Iceland.

"Hjorleif was driven further west until he landed on a headland where he built two homesteads. He lived there during the winter and decided to sow a corn crop in the spring. Although he had an ox, he made his slaves pull the plough. They plotted amongst themselves and killed the ox, telling Hjorleif that a bear had done

*These pillars were carved in the shape of the gods and were regarded as sacred.

A volcano and the sort of harsh landscape the Vikings found in Iceland

Iceland was a land of volcanoes, hot water geysers and boiling mud, of icesheets and glaciers, and of mountains and forests. But the hills and valleys near the sea had good pastures for sheep and cattle, and the lakes and rivers were full of trout and salmon. By 930, some 50,000 Vikings were living on the island. Their lives were hard, their tempers short and their actions violent.

Greenland adventure

One of the settlers, Erik the Red, was outlawed for three years for killing some men. He sailed further west in search of a new land (982): "Erik put out to sea past Snaefells Glacier and sailed on until he sighted land near a glacier called Blaserk. He sailed south from there to see if the land was fit to live in. He spent two more years exploring the country. In the summer of the third year, he sailed back to Iceland. He named the land he had discovered 'Greenland', for he said that people would be more tempted to go there if it had an attractive name. Erik spent the winter in Iceland. Next summer, he set off to colonize Greenland, and he made his home at Brattahlid (141)."

Greenland must have been a great disappointment to the new colonists: it was even icier and more barren than Iceland. Nevertheless, two settlements developed, one on the east coast and the other on the west coast. Eventually, some 3,000 people made their homes there, exporting furs and hides, ropes and cables, oils, woollens and sea ivory, not to mention polar bears and falcons. The Greenlanders were great traders and fishermen; they wandered further west and discovered America in about 986.

Vinland: the discovery of America

The discovery was made by a man called Bjarni on a voyage from Iceland to Greenland: "They put to sea as soon as they were ready and sailed for three days until land was lost to sight below the horizon. Then the fair wind failed and northerly winds and fog set in, and for many days they had no idea what their course was. After that they saw the sun again and were able to get their bearings; they hoisted sail and after a day's sailing they sighted land. They discussed among themselves what country this might be. Bjarni said that he thought it could not be Greenland (142)."

Probably the land that Bjarni sighted but did not explore was Baffin Island. He made no effort to follow up his discovery, this was left to Leif Eriksson, the son of the founder of the Greenland colony. In 1000, he bought Bjarni's *knarr*, collected a crew of thirty-five brave men and set off in search of this new land:

"The first landfall they made was the country that Bjarni had sighted last. They sailed right up to the shore and cast anchor, then they lowered a boat and landed. There was grass to be seen, and the hinterland was covered with great glaciers, and between the glaciers and the shore, the land was like one great slab of rock. It seemed to them a worthless country. *Leif Eriksson*

"They returned to their ship and put to sea, and sighted a second land. Once again they sailed right up to it. This country was flat and wooded, with white sandy beaches wherever they went; and the land sloped gently down to the sea. Leif said, 'This country shall be named Markland' [Forest Land, probably Labrador].

"They hurried back to their ship as quickly as possible and sailed away before a north-east wind for two days until they sighted land again . . . They went ashore and looked around them. The weather was fine. There was dew on the grass, and the first thing they did was to get some of it on their hands and put it to their lips—it seemed to them the sweetest thing they had ever tasted (143)." [This was probably Belle Island off Newfoundland.]

They steered a westerly course and came to some shallows where they were left high and dry when the tide went out. Later, they refloated the ship and anchored off the coast. Here they built some shacks in which to spend the winter: "There was no lack of salmon in the river or the lake, bigger salmon than they had ever seen. The country seemed so favourable to them that no winter fodder would be needed for the livestock. There was no frost all winter and the grass hardly withered at all (144)."

In the spring, they discovered wild vines and cut down plenty of timber to take back with them to Greenland. Leif named the place Vinland, or Wine-land. The next voyage was led by Leif's brother, Thorvold. During their explorations, they came across some Indians, whom they called Skraelings, and killed them. The angry tribe counter-attacked with a fleet of canoes. The Vikings tried to protect themselves by fixing their shields to the sides of the ship, but Thorvold was mortally wounded. The survivors beat off the attack and returned home next year with another cargo of timber and grapes. *Thorvold*

Thorfinn Karlsefni led a fourth voyage in a serious attempt to *Karlsefni*

Overleaf Erik the Red discovers Greenland (A.D. 982)

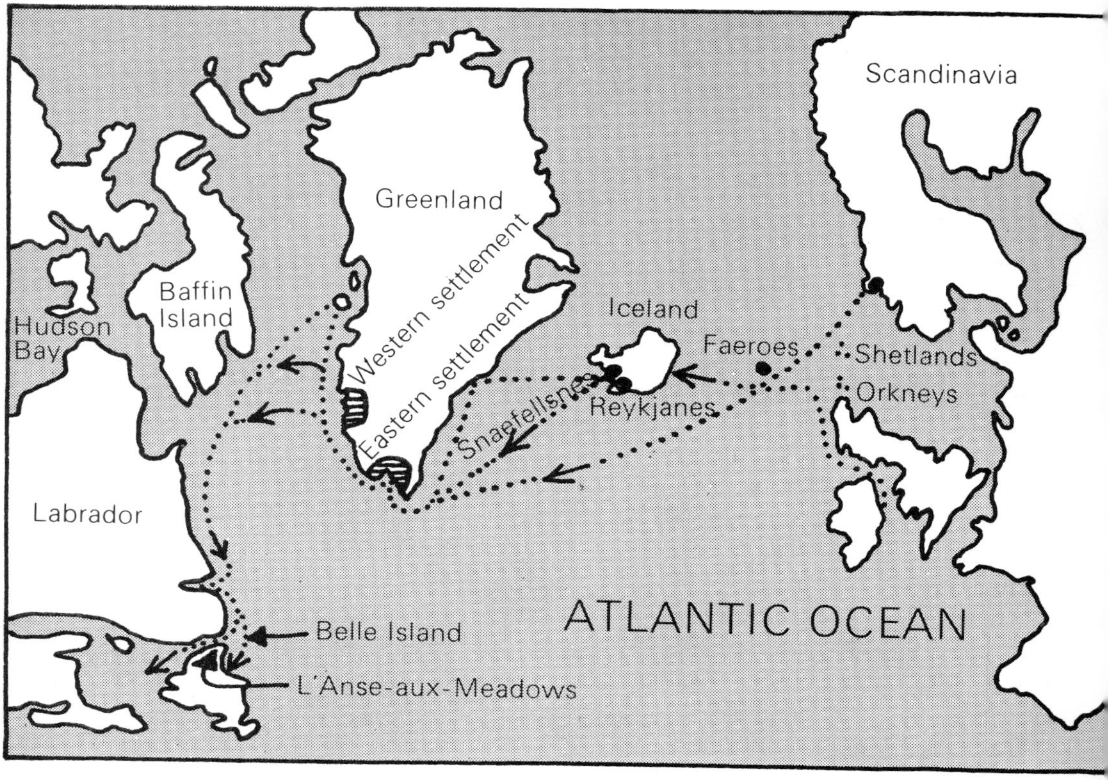

The Atlantic voyages of the Vikings

found a colony in the new lands. Some 160 men and women and "all kinds of livestock" set off in three ships. They made their way to Vinland and spent their first winter, a difficult one, in Leif's houses. They were very short of food and made themselves ill by eating a whale that was washed up on the beach. Some of the would-be settlers were so disgusted by their experiences that they insisted on going home. They missed Greenland and were cast away on the shores of Ireland where they were either killed or enslaved.

The rest sailed further south until they came to a landlocked bay they called "Hope" (probably somewhere in Newfoundland):

"That spring, Karlsefni and his men sailed a long way down the coast until they came to a river which flowed from the land into a lake and then into the sea. There were such large sandbanks at its mouth that they could only get into the river at high tide. Ashore they found fields of self-sown corn on the low-lying land and vines wherever there were woods. Every stream was full of fish. Below high water mark they dug trenches in the sand, so that when the tide went out there were halibut stranded in the pools. There were vast numbers of every kind of animal in the forest. They spent a fortnight there enjoying themselves and noticed nothing strange.

"Then, early one morning, they saw a large number of canoes approaching full of Skraelings who were waving things like flails in the air [probably ceremonial rattles]. 'What does this mean?' asked Karlsefni. 'Maybe it is a sign of peace,' replied Snorri, 'so let's take out a white shield and show it to them.' They did this and their visitors paddled towards them. They were dark skinned, ugly men with untidy coarse hair. They had large eyes and were broad in the cheek. They stayed there for a time and then paddled off round the headland (145)."

Trouble with the Indians

The Vikings spent the winter there. No snow fell, so the animals were able to graze in the open the whole time. Then, in the spring: "They saw a large number of canoes paddling towards them once more. The flails were waved in each boat and Karlsefni and his men raised their shields and they traded together. Most of the Skraelings wanted to buy red cloth and offered furs and skins in return. They also wanted swords but Karlsefni would not allow his men to sell them.

"Next moment, the bull belonging to Karlsefni and his men rushed out of the forest bellowing loudly. The Skraelings were so terrified that they raced back to their canoes and paddled away. Nothing more was seen or heard of them for three weeks. Then, a great fleet of canoes came up the river from the south. This time the flails were waved about in a different way and all the Skraelings were yelling so fiercely that Karlsefni and his men took out their red shields. The Skraelings leapt from their canoes, charged at the Vikings and they fought together. There was a heavy shower of stones, as the Skraelings had slings. Karlsefni and his men saw the Skraelings hoisting a large blue-black ball up a pole which made a hideous noise when they released it. The Vikings were terrified and ran away hoping to escape along the river. They ran until they reached some rocks where they defended themselves bravely. They were saved by a woman called Freydis who seized a sword and frightened the Skraelings away (146)."

Karlsefni and his people decided to pack up and go home. They liked the land well enough, but realized that there could be no peace with the Skraelings. They sailed north and spent another winter in Vinland before sailing to Greenland.

Vikings in Newfoundland

On this voyage, they may have reached as far south as Newfoundland. There, Dr. Helge Ingstad has excavated the sites of two long houses at L'Anse-aux-Meadows. Tests have indicated a date of 1000—plus or minus 100 years—for the site. The halls have firepits and raised earth benches. There is a primitive ironworks and a steam bath. Dr. Ingstad believes that 75 to 90 people may have lived there at one time.

Decline of the Atlantic colonies

The sagas tell of later attempts to settle Vinland, but none of them succeeded, although ships from Greenland were still visiting Markland as late as 1347 in search of timber. For a time the Greenlanders were very successful and had their own national assembly, the Althing. But in 1261 they were taken over by the Norwegians who made trade with Greenland a royal monopoly. Fewer and fewer ships visited them. First the Western Settlement collapsed, and the Eastern Settlement was left to struggle on alone. Gradually, the climate changed and ice-floes blocked the fjords. As the Greenlanders weakened, the Eskimos closed in and wiped them out. The only trace of the Settlements that a visitor to southwest Greenland found in 1540 was a "dead man lying face downwards on the ground. He was wearing a hood and clothes made of coarse woollens and sealskin. Beside him lay a knife, badly bent and almost worn away (147)."

Even the Icelanders fell on evil days. Here too the ice closed in and much good farm land was ruined by an eruption of Mount Hekla in 1300. By this time the great sagas had been written. The sagas are stories embodying the history of an Icelandic family or a Norwegian king. The greatest of them, like "Egil's Saga," "Laxdaela Saga" and "Njal's Saga," were written in the thirteenth century. The "Saga Age" was brought to an end by natural calamities and the Black Death epidemic of 1349 which killed at least a third of the population. Hardly any ships reached them from Norway, and they lacked the timber to build many of their own. Nevertheless, the hardy Icelanders survived until better days, thanks to their herds of cattle, flocks of sheep, and the fish from the sea, lakes and rivers.

9 Conclusion: The End of the Viking Era

End of an era

BY ABOUT 1066, the great days of the Vikings were over. The raids continued for some time, but were increasingly ineffective. What had happened?

Important social changes had taken place in the Scandinavian communities. In early Viking times there had been many petty kings whose power was confined to their immediate estates. But as the years passed, effective kingdoms were created by strong men like Olaf Tryggvason and Swein Forkbeard. The chieftains, who had played one king off against another, and gone raiding whenever they chose, found themselves reduced to the status of the king's representatives.

Coming of Christianity

The struggle between the kings and the chieftains usually coincided with the battle between paganism and Christianity. Denmark was the first Scandinavian kingdom to be converted. Harald Bluetooth (945–985) was convinced of the power of Jesus by a brave little priest called Poppo who "picked up red hot iron bars and showed his unscorched hands to the King. Thereafter, King Harald and the whole Danish army were baptised (148)."

King Hakon (945–960) was the first Christian King of Norway. But he had to tread carefully: "He was a good Christian when he came to Norway, but all the land was heathen and as he needed the help and friendship of the people, he decided to conceal his Christianity. When he had established himself in the land and fully subjected it to himself, he sent to England for a bishop and other priests (149)." Norway's conversion was completed by Olaf Tryggvason (995–1000) and St. Olaf (1014–30) who used terrorist methods.

Left An example of a beautifully-made Viking gold ornament *above* and a Viking wood carving *below*

The Swedes clung tenaciously to the old faith. An Anglo-Danish monk wrote gloomily at the beginning of the twelfth century: "As long as things go well, Svear and Goter seem willing to honour Christianity, but when they go wrong and there are bad harvests, droughts, storms, enemy attacks or outbreaks of fire, they persecute the Church they nominally support, not only with words but in deeds. They revenge themselves upon the Christians and seek to chase them right out of the country (150)." Gradually, the Christian priests won and the old religion disappeared. Scandinavia was divided up into bishoprics and parishes and the bishops and priests supported the kings who were their protectors and kept law and order.

Population movement ended

The great overseas migration of the Vikings was over. There was nowhere left to colonize—the Western Islands, Iceland and Greenland were fully settled. However, Scandinavian farming methods had improved and more land was brought under cultivation. At last they were able to satisfy their own needs.

Meanwhile, the Norse colonists in Ireland, the English Danelaw, Normandy and Russia were being absorbed by the native populations. They married the local girls and accepted the religion, language and customs of their adopted countries.

Raiding became more difficult: the rulers of Western Europe were stronger in the eleventh century than they had been in the ninth. Everywhere, Viking armies were being bloodily defeated. One of the most celebrated of these defeats took place at Clontarf in Ireland at the hands of the aged Brian Boru in 1014: "On one side of the battle were the shouting, hard hearted, murderous Vikings. They had sharp, poisoned arrows which had been dipped in the blood of dragons, toads, scorpions and venomous snakes of all kinds. They were equipped with fine quivers and polished, shining yellow bows and strong spears. They wore heavy coats of mail of double refined iron and carried stout swords.

Battle of Clontarf

"On the other side were the brave Irishmen—the lions, wolfhounds and hawks of Ireland. They had spears and shields, broad axes and swords. They wore golden crested helmets and fine cloth tunics and shirts of many colours.

"When the battle began, Brian had his cushions spread upon the ground, opened his prayer book, put his hands together and prayed. The fighting continued from sunrise to sunset . . . At the end of the day, the Irish gathered themselves for one last great effort and swept the Vikings from the field. In the excitement, the King's guards rushed off and joined in the killing.

"Then, three Vikings led by Earl Brodir approached the King. Brian arose and unsheathed his great two-handed sword. Brodir carried a gleaming battleaxe in his hand. He passed Brian without noticing him, but one of his men called out, 'This is the High King.' 'No,' said Earl Brodir, 'no, that is not he, but a noble priest.' 'By your leave,' insisted the soldier, 'that is Brian the High King.' At that, Brian struck Brodir with his sword and cut off his left leg and right foot. At the very same moment, the Viking dealt Brian a blow with his axe which cut off the King's head. Both fell dead to the ground (151)."

Viking legacy

What had the Viking peoples achieved? Traditionally, historians have followed contemporary chroniclers and described them as barbarians who robbed, raped and murdered their way across Europe, wantonly destroying fine buildings and beautiful works of art. The Vikings did these things, but so did the other Europeans when they were fighting among themselves. What marked the Vikings out for special treatment by the chroniclers was their paganism.

On the credit side, the Vikings stimulated trade wherever they went and founded or developed thriving towns. Often, they taught the local people new skills like shipbuilding and coin making. The Vikings developed a distinctive art style, as anyone who looks at their swords, wood carvings and metal work can see. They produced a fine heroic literature—the Sagas—which forms part of our cultural heritage in the West.

Even their attacks had some value, since they forced their victims to stand together. For example, the Viking raids provided the stimulus for the conquest of England by the kings of Wessex and for the unification of the Slav tribes by the Rus.

Lastly, wherever they settled, they kept alive their own sense of personal freedom—when the Franks asked the Vikings who their leader was, they answered proudly, "We have no lord, we are all equal (152)."

For two and a half centuries, the Vikings had terrorized Europe, But now people suddenly asked (153):

What has become of the warrior?
What has become of the steed?
What has become of the seats at the banquet?
Where are the joys of the hall?
O for the bright cup.
O for the mailclad warrior.
O for the glory of the prince.
Now that time has passed away
And grown dark under the cover of night
As if it had never been.

Glossary

ADZE A tool for cutting away the surface of wood; like an axe with an arched blade at right angles to the handle.

BURGH Borough.

CAULK To stop up the cracks between the planks of a ship with waterproof material to prevent leakages.

CUDGEL A short, thick stick used as a weapon.

EMIR The title given to a Muslim ruler.

GUILE Clever or crafty behaviour.

HARRIED Harassed.

LIBATION A drink-offering to a god.

LOOT To steal money or goods.

PILLAGE To rob a town of anything of value, especially during a war.

PLUNDER To systematically rob any valuables from a town by force.

POMMEL The knob at the top of a sword.

SACK The plundering of a place by an army, usually involving destruction and killing.

SIEGE WARFARE The method of capturing a fortified place by surrounding it, cutting its lines of supply and then attacking it with weapons.

SLAY Kill.

SPOOR The track or scent of an animal.

WITHIES Ropes of twisted twigs or stems used to bind things together.

ZENITH The point in the heavens directly above the observer.

Some Important Dates

793	Vikings attack Lindisfarne on the English coast.
844	Vikings reach Spain for the first time, but are routed by the Moors.
845	Ragnar Hairy-Breeches besieges Paris.
859–62	Bjorn and Hastings make a raid into the Mediterranean.
860	First Viking attack on Constantinople.
867	The sons of Ragnar Hairy-Breeches invade England.
870(?)	Vikings discover Iceland.
878	Alfred the Great defeats Guthrum at the Battle of Edington (Treaty of Chippenham).
885	Siegfried and his Great Army besiege Paris.
893	The Great Army invades England.
911	Treaty of St. Claire-sur-Epte: the Viking Rollo becomes the first Duke of Normandy.
912	The Rus (Vikings in Russia) pillage the lands around the Caspian Sea.
937	The Battle of Brunanbugh; Athelstan defeats the Scots and Vikings.
982	Erik the Red discovers Greenland.
986	Bjarni sights Vinland.
991	The Battle of Maldon; the defeat of Earl Brihtnoth.
1000	Thorfinn Karlsefni voyages to Vinland.
	The Battle of Svolder; the death of Olaf Tryggvason.
1002	The Massacre of St. Brice's Day.
1009	Olaf the Stout destroys London Bridge.
1014	The Battle of Clontarf; Brian Boru defeats the

	Vikings in Ireland.
1017	Canute is elected King of England.
1028	The Battle of Stiklarstadir; Canute defeats Olaf the Stout and wins control of Norway.
1066	Death of Edward the Confessor.
	The Battle of Stamford Bridge, and death of Harald Hardradi.
	The Battle of Hastings, the victory of Duke William of Normandy over the English.
1170–1250	The great age of saga writing in Iceland.
1261	Greenland is taken over by the Norwegians; the decline of the Western and Eastern Settlements.
1347	The last recorded voyage to Markland.

Further Reading

Modern historians are rethinking their attitudes towards the Vikings; much new evidence has been found from the study of place names and archaeology. Yet our knowledge of these peoples is still firmly based upon contemporary chronicles, and on the great sagas written two or three hundred years after the events described. We can now read many of the sagas in translation; the Penguin Classics Series includes *Njal's Saga*, the *Laxdaela, King Harald's Saga* and the *Vinland Sagas*; the Everyman Library contains *Snorri Sturlason's Heimskringla* (Sagas of the Norse Kings), the *Saga of Burnt Njal*, and the *Saga of Grettir the Strong*. Selections from many sources are to be found in Volume I and II of *English Historical Documents* (Eyre & Spottiswoode, 1955), and the *Early Middle Ages* (Hutchinson's Portraits and Documents Series, 1966). The easiest available chronicle is the *Anglo-Saxon Chronicle* (Everyman Library, 1960).

GENERAL SURVEYS

G. Jones, *The Vikings* (Oxford, 1968)
H. Arbman, *The Vikings* (Ancient Peoples and Places; Thames & Hudson, 1961)
J. Brondsted, *The Vikings* (Penguin, 1960)
P. H. Sawyer, *The Age of the Vikings* (Arnold, 1971)
Peter Brent, *The Viking Saga* (Weidenfeld and Nicolson, 1975)
Magnus Magnusson, *Vikings!* (Bodley Head, 1980)

REGIONAL STUDIES

K. Larsen, *A History of Norway* (Princeton, 1948)
K. Gjerset, *History of Iceland* (London, 1923)
P. Norlund, *Viking Settlers in Greenland* (Cambridge, 1936)
P. H. Blair, *Introduction to Anglo-Saxon England* (Cambridge, 1956)
G. Vernadsky, *The Origins of Russia* (Clarendon Press, 1959)

SPECIAL THEMES

J. Simpson, *Everyday Life in the Viking Age* (Batsford-Putnam, 1967)
A. W. Brogger and H. Shetelig, *The Viking Ships* (Oslo, 1950)
H. R. E. Davidson, *Gods and Myths of Northern Europe* (Penguin, 1964)
R. W. V. Elliott, *Runes* (Manchester University Press, 1959)
D. M. Wilson and O. Klindt-Jensen, *Viking Art* (Allen & Unwin, 1966)

FOR YOUNG PEOPLE

D. R. Barker, *Vikings at Home and Abroad* (Arnold, 1966)
R. L. Green, *The Saga of Asgard* (Puffin, 1960)
G. L. Proctor, *The Vikings* (Longmans Then & There Series, 1959)
M. Reeves, *Alfred and the Danes* (Longmans Then & There Series, 1959)
Sheila Ferguson, *Growing Up in Viking Times* (Batsford, 1981)
Christopher Gibb, *A Viking Sailor* (Wayland, 1982)

List of Sources

The author has substituted words and rearranged sentences in most of the extracts to facilitate easy understanding.

(1) Symeon of Durham. *History of the Kings*, ed. J. Stevenson (1855)

(2) Adam of Bremen. *Gesta Hammaburgensis Ecclesiae Pontificum*, trans. F. J. Tschan. 1959

(3) *Ibid*

(4) *Ibid*

(5) Notker the Stammerer. *Charlemagne*, trans. L. Thorpe. 1969

(6) *The War of the Gaedil with the Gaill*, trans. & ed. J. H. Todd. Rolls Series, 1867

(7) Ibn Miskawaih, trans. C. A. Macartney, *The Magyars of the Ninth Century*, 1930

(8) *Magnus Barefoot's Saga*, trans. P. B. du Chaillu, *The Viking Age*, 1889

(9) Saxo Grammaticus, *Gesta Danorum*, trans. Oliver Elton, 1894

(10) *Njal's Saga*, P. B. du Chaillu, *op. cit.*

(11) *Ibid*

(12) *Volsunga Saga*, trans. P. B. du Chaillu, *The Viking Age*, 1889

(13) *Sturlang Starfsami's Saga*, *ibid*

(14) *Orvar Odd's Saga*, *ibid*

(15) Snorre Sturlason, *Heimskringla*, trans. Samuel Laing, revised by R. B. Anderson (John C. Nimmo, 1889)

(16) *St. Olaf's Saga*, *ibid*

(17) *Ynglinga Saga*, P. B. du Chaillu, *op. cit.*

(18) *St. Olaf's Saga*, Snorre Sturlason, *op. cit.*

(19) *Harald Hardradi's Saga*, trans. S. Laing, *op. cit.*

(20) a. *Rigsmal*; b. *Njal's Saga*; c. *Laxdaela Saga* trans. P. B. du Chaillu, *op. cit.*

(21) a. *Gunnlaug Ormstunga*; b. *Kjalnesinga Saga*, *ibid*

(22) *Njal's Saga*, P. B. du Chaillu, *op. cit.*

(23) *Eyrbyggja*, *ibid*

(24) *Konungs Skuggsja*, *ibid*

(25) *Elder Edda*, *ibid*

(26) *An Bogsveigi's Saga*, *ibid*

(27) Al-Tartushi from Ibrahim ibn Jakub's *Travel Book*, quoted by Gwyn Jones, *The Vikings*, 1968

(28) *Fagrskinna*, trans. P. B. du Chaillu, *op. cit.*

(29) *Grettir's Saga*, *ibid*

(30) *Egil's Saga*, *ibid*

(31) *Egil's Saga*, *ibid*

(32) *Orkneyingers' Saga*, *Icelandic Sagas III*, trans. Sir G. W. Dasent, 1894, Rolls Series No. 88

(33) *Egil's Saga*, trans. P. B. du Chaillu, *op. cit.*

(34) *A Literal English Translation of King Alfred's Anglo-Saxon Version of the Compendious History of the World by Orosius* by Rev. J. Boswoth, 1855

(35) *Faereyinga Saga*, trans. P. B. du Chaillu, *op. cit.*

(36) *Al-Tartushi*, quoted Gwyn Jones, *op. cit.*

(37) Rigsmal, *Corpus Poeticum Boreale*, trans. Vigfusson & Powell, 1883

(38) *Frostathing Law*, trans. P. B. du Chaillu, *op. cit.*

(39) *Laxdaela Saga*, *ibid*

(40) *Hervara Saga*, *ibid*

(41) *Laxdaela Saga*, *ibid*

(42) *Grettir's Saga, ibid*
(43) *Volsunga Saga, ibid*
(44) *Frostathing Law, ibid*
(45) *Harald Hardradi's Saga, ibid*
(46) J. Brondsted, *The Vikings*, 1960
(47) *Ibid*
(48) *Ibid*
(49) *Hrolf Kraki's Saga*, trans. P. B. du Chaillu, *op. cit.*
(50) *St. Olaf's Saga, ibid*
(51) *Olaf Tryggvason's Saga, ibid*
(52) *Frostathing Law, ibid*
(53) *Ynglinga Saga, ibid*
(54) *Ibid*
(55) *Thorstein of the Cudgel Blow's Saga*, quoted in J. Simpson, *Everyday life in the Viking Age*, 1967
(56) *Sigurd Jorsalafar's Saga*, trans. P. B. du Chaillu, *op. cit.*
(57) *Ibid*
(58) J. Simpson, *op. cit.*
(59) Ibn Rustah, trans. C. A. Macartney, *op. cit.*
(60) *Gulathing Law*, trans. P. B. du Chaillu, *op. cit.*
(61) *Havamal, ibid*
(62) *Later Edda, ibid*
(63) *Ynglinga Saga, ibid*
(64) *Later Edda, ibid*
(65) *Ynglinga Saga, ibid*
(66) Adam of Bremen, *op. cit.*
(67) Ibn Fadlan, trans. H. M. Smyser, *Medieval and Linguistic Studies in Honour of Francis Peabody Magoun*, N.Y., 1965
(68) *Erik's Saga*, trans. M. Magnusson and Palsson, *The Vinland Sagas*, 1965
(69) Ibn Rustah, trans. C. A. Macartney, *op. cit.*
(70) Ibn Fadlan, trans. H. M. Smyser, *op. cit.*
(71) *Ibid*
(72) *Ibid*
(73) Snorri Sturlason, trans. S. Laing, *op. cit.*
(74) Tacitus, *On Britain and Germany*, trans. H. Mattingly, Penguin Classics, 1948
(75) *Olaf Tryggvason's Saga*, trans. S. Laing, *op. cit.*
(76) *Flateyjarbok*, trans. P. B. du Chaillu, *op. cit.*
(77) J. Simpson, *op. cit.*
(78) *Njal's Saga*, trans. P. B. du Chaillu, *op. cit.*
(79) *Svarfdaela Saga, ibid*
(80) *Egil's Saga, ibid*
(81) *Fridthjof's Saga, ibid*
(82) *Flateyjarbok, ibid*
(83) *Landnamabok*, trans. T. Ellwood, *The Book of the Settlement*, 1898
(84) *Olaf Tryggvason's Saga*, trans. S. Laing, *op. cit.*
(85) *Anglo-Saxon Chronicle*, trans. D. Whitelock, *English Historical Documents*, Vol. I, 1955
(86) Asser, *Life of Alfred*, ed. J. Stevenson, 1854
(87) *Anglo-Saxon Chronicle*, trans. D. Whitelock, *op. cit.*
(88) *Ibid*
(89) Asser, *op. cit.*
(90) *Anglo-Saxon Chronicle*, trans. D. Whitelock, *op. cit.*
(91) William of Malmesbury, *Chronicle of the Kings of England*, trans. John Sharpe, 1815
(92) *Anglo-Saxon Chronicle*, trans. D. Whitelock, *op. cit.*
(93) *Ibid*
(94) *Ibid*
(95) *Ibid*
(96) *Ibid*
(97) *Ibid*
(98) *Ibid*
(99) *Ibid*
(100) *Edgar the Peaceable's Laws*, trans. D. Whitelock, *op. cit.*
(101) *Anglo-Saxon Chronicle*, trans. D. Whitelock, *op. cit.*
(102) *Battle of Maldon*, trans. D. Whitelock, *op. cit.*
(103) *Anglo-Saxon Chronicle*, trans. D. Whitelock, *op. cit.*
(104) *Cartulary of St. Fridewide, ibid*
(105) *St. Olaf's Saga*, trans. S. Laing, *op. cit.*
(106) *Anglo-Saxon Chronicle*, trans. D. Whitelock, *op. cit.*
(107) *Knytlinga Saga*, trans. P. B. du Chaillu, *op. cit.*
(108) *Harald Hardradi's Saga*, trans. S. Laing, *op. cit.*
(109) *Ibid*
(110) *Anglo-Saxon Chronicle*, D. C. Douglas & G. W. Greenway, *English Historical Documents*, Vol. II, 1955
(111) *Ibid*
(112) *Annals of St. Bertin*, trans. P. B. du Chaillu, *op. cit.*
(113) Ibn Kutia, trans. Jon Stefansson, *Saga Book of the Viking Club*, Vol. VI, 1908–9
(114) *Ibid*

(115) *Annals of St. Bertin*, trans P. B. du Chaillu, *op. cit.*
(116) *Ibid*
(117) Ermantarius of Noirmoutier, quoted by Gwyn Jones, *op. cit.*
(118) Ibn Adhari, trans. Jon Stefansson, *op. cit.*
(119) Roger of Wendover, *Flowers of History*, trans. J. A. Giles, Bohn's Antiquarian Library, 1849
(120) Ibn Adhari, trans. Jon Stefansson, *op. cit.*
(121) Abbo of Fleury, trans. P. B. du Chaillu, *op. cit.*
(122) *Ibid*
(123) *Ibid*
(124) *Ibid*
(125) *Harald Fairhair's Saga*, trans. S. Laing, *op. cit.*
(126) William of Jumierges, *Gesta Normannorum Ducum*, trans. by author
(127) *The Russian Primary Chronicle*, trans. Samuel H. Cross, Harvard Studies and Notes in Philology and Literature, Vol. XII, 1930
(128) Ibn Rustah, trans. C. A. Macartney, *op. cit.*
(129) Constantine Porphyrogenitus, *De Administrando Imperio*, trans. R. J. Jenkins, *Magyargorog tanul manyok*, No. 29, 1949
(130) *Ibid*
(131) *Ibid*
(132) Hudud-al-'Alam, trans. V. E. Minorsky, *E. W. Gibb Memorial Publications*, New Series XI, 1937
(133) *The Works of Liuprand of Cremona*, trans. F. A. Wright, Broadway Medieval Library
(134) *Russian Primary Chronicle*, trans. S. H. Cross, *op. cit.*
(135) Ibn Fadlan, trans. H. M. Smyser, *op. cit.*
(136) *Ibid*
(137) Al Masudi's *Meadows of Gold and Mines of Gems*, trans. A. Spenger, 1841
(138) *Egil's Saga*, trans. P. B du Chaillu, *op. cit.*
(139) *Landnamabok*, trans. T. Ellwood, *op. cit.*
(140) *Ibid*
(141) *Graenlendinga Saga*, trans. M. Magnusson & H. Palsson, *op. cit.*
(142) *Ibid*
(143) *Ibid*
(144) *Ibid*
(145) *Erik's Saga*, trans. Gwyn Jones, *Erik the Red and other Icelandic Sagas*, 1961
(146) *Ibid*
(147) Quoted in D. R. Barker, *Vikings at Home and Abroad*, 1966
(148) *Olaf Tryggvason's Saga*, trans. S. Laing, *op. cit.*
(149) *Hakon the Good's Saga*, trans. P. B. du Chaillu, *op. cit.*
(150) *Aelnoth of Canterbury*, quoted by J. Brondsted, *op. cit.*
(151) *The War of the Gaedil with the Gaill*, trans. J. H. Todd, *op. cit.*
(152) William of Jumierges, *op. cit.*
(153) D. Whitelock, *op. cit.*

PICTURE CREDITS

The Publishers wish to thank the following for permission to reproduce the illustrations on the pages mentioned: the Mansell Collection, *jacket*, *frontispiece*, 4, 20–21, 48, 51, 54, 56, 58–59, 62, 71, 76–77, 86, 92, 110–111; Mats Wibe Lund Jr, 14, 28, 106–107; Universitetets Oldsaksamling Oslo, 16, 17 *(left)*, 19, 29, (30 *(above)*, 36–37, 116; London Museum, 17 *(right)*, 23; National Museum, Copenhagen, 26, 30 *(below)*; Iceland Tourist Information Bureau, 27; Swedish National Travel Association, 39; National Museum of Antiquities of Scotland, 40; Radio Times Hulton Picture Library, 44, 104–105; Carlsberg Glyptotek, 47; Real Biblioteca del Escorian, 78; MAS, Barcelona, 80; Stiftsbibliothek St. Gallen, 83; Victoria and Albert Museum, 97; Biblioteca Apostolica Vaticana, 98–99. Other illustrations appearing in this book are the property of the Wayland Picture Library.

Index